A LIFE

·with·

·from ASTON to FACEL VEGA·
Fred Hobbs

A **FOULIS** Motoring Book

First published 1990
© Fred Hobbs 1990

Published by:
Haynes Publishing Group
Sparkford, Nr Yeovil
Somerset BA22 7JJ, England

Haynes Publications Inc
861 Lawrence Drive, Newbury Park,
California 91320, USA

British Library Cataloguing in Publication Data
Hobbs, Fred
A life with HWM: from Alta to Facel Vega.
1. Great Britain. Car industries. Companies, history
I. Title
338.7'6292222'0941
ISBN 0-85429-718-9

Library of Congress Catalog Card Number
89-81503

Editor: Robin Read
Typeset in Times med roman 11/12pt
Printed in England by J.H. Haynes & Co. Ltd.

CONTENTS

FOREWORD

The author of this book joined me just after the war when we were both discharged from the RAF.

A large part of Fred Hobbs' life was spent at HWM and most of the book is devoted to his time there.

From the beginning we specialised in sports, racing and luxury cars and here is a chronicle of his remarkable experiences as Works Manager and then as Works Director. They were good times; Fred and I shared many experiences and, in his book, he has succeeded in capturing the atmosphere of the period.

My experience is that the type of cars that we had always had problems, but Fred was utterly invaluable in solving them.

It is sad to think that, except for the Aston Martin, most of the exotic cars that we handled are with us no more.

How privileged we are to have lived through those times.

George Abecassis

The Author with his E-type at a Jaguar Drivers Club Meeting. The photograph originally appeared in an article in the Surrey Herald newspaper claiming "you are never too old to drive an E-type". Fred Hobbs attributes his continuing excellent health to regular exercise at the wheel of such superb motoring thoroughbreds as this

AUTHOR'S NOTE

I have been tempted to write this book because, over the years, the personal narratives of other people have provided me with much enjoyment and some of my friends have kindly suggested that my own life story might provide similar pleasure to others.

The big difference is that the other books have been written by people who are famous, or at least well known. Unfortunately, I can make no claim to fame and outside my own circle must be virtually unknown.

This being so, it is possibly presumptuous of me to assume that anyone will be interested in my story. On the other hand, it is also possible some people will enjoy reading about an ordinary sort of bloke who, from very humble beginnings, has managed to achieve a modest amount of success and, in the process, has accumulated a wealth of experience. I can only wait and see. With the exception of a few technical details which I had to look up, the whole story has been written from memory. As we all know, this can be a bit fickle at times, especially as one gets older, but I have tried hard to only put in things I can remember with certainty. Nevertheless, if any errors have crept in I hope I will be forgiven. I am grateful for all the encouragement I have received and would like to acknowledge the assistance given by the Editors of *Motor Sport, The Jaguar Driver* and *Faceletter*. Their kind permission for me to use extracts from some of the articles I have written for them has been of great help, saving me the necessity of thinking up those particular episodes again.

My thanks also to Keith Hopkins, Emma Anderson and various others who have been of help and most of all to Tricia Price who so valiantly translated my handwriting into a beautifully typed manuscript. I have enjoyed writing it. I hope you enjoy reading it.

Fred Hobbs

1
THE VERY EARLY DAYS

For some unexplained reason I was hooked on motor cars as soon as I was born. It did not run in the family – my father still lived mentally in the horse and carriage age and hated them – but as soon as I was old enough to recognise shapes and sounds, draw rough pictures. etc., they were my main interest in life. I was given a copy of *The Autocar 1919 Show Report* when I was five years old and still have it.

We lived in Shepperton, then a country village. Our cottage was nowhere near the road, but I used to long for the day when I would be old enough to walk down the lane to the main road and watch the cars go by. Mind you, if one car an hour went by it was a big deal!

There was still romance in motoring then although we were well past the 'early days'. The First World War had only been over for a short time and, although technical advances had been made, the roads and general conditions were very much as they had been in 1914. In my own little village we only had one main road which went right through it. The side roads were narrow and of poor quality, some of them little more than lanes passing through or adjacent to fields. There was one I particularly remember, called, for reasons that escape me now, Cut Throat Lane. This was reached over a stile and was rich in rare wild flowers, butterflies and blackberry bushes. For decades now this has been an important through road, carrying so much traffic there are plans afoot to make it dual carriageway.

The cars themselves were all pre-war until the early twenties when normal production commenced. New models from existing manufacturers appeared together with many new makes, some good solid cars, some dreadful contraptions, as small companies sought to cash in on the expected post war boom. Most of these, good and bad were doomed to failure within the next few years.

Of course, all this meant nothing to me. A motor car, any motor car, drew me like a magnet and before long I could recognise all the various makes. I started collecting numbers and it soon became evident that I was seeing the same one several times a day, a Renault landaulette, beautiful in dark red with masses of shiny brass. This obviously required investigation and I soon discovered it was the local taxi owned by old Bill Howard, the village cabbie, who had reluctantly given up his horse drawn vehicle. From then on my future was settled even at the tender age of six I realised I would have to earn my living one day, and what better way to do it than by being a taxi driver?

Another car to hold my attention was a 1914 Argyle open tourer in dark green, all brass fittings, a boa constrictor horn and electric lighting. This car was housed in the old stable of a big house on the main road and by good fortune our garden backed on to it. I used to wait for the owner to come home and watch him put it away. He would often chat to me and I learned it had sleeve valves. I had no idea what valves were, sleeve or otherwise, but it seemed an important point and I was proud to share the knowledge. One day I had nipped over the wall scrumping walnuts. The stable door was open and I saw some stairs leading up to a loft. I decided to hide in the loft, wait for the car to come in and then climb down to have a good look at it when the owner had gone indoors. After a while it suddenly struck me he would lock the doors after him and I would be trapped there all night. Terrified, I flew down the stairs and back over the wall, just having time to regain my composure before he came in. And I didn't even get my walnuts!

It was some years before I had a chance to actually ride in a car, a 1913 Napier which had been fitted with a new landaulette body in 1919 or 20. It belonged to Whiteley Village, a small self-contained community for old people set in lovely surroundings and administered by a Trust set up by William Whiteley of London store fame. It is still there, as immaculate as ever and a delightful place to live out one's age. They also had a Lacre bus, the only vehicle of this make I can remember seeing. It had solid tyres and chain drive and I've no idea how old it was. Every Saturday evening the chauffeur had to drive to the station, a distance of about a mile, to meet the London train. Usually he took the Napier but if there were a number of people to pick up he would take the bus.

Through my parents I was friendly with him and as soon as I could ride a bike I would cycle the eight miles to his house and go with him. His wife usually gave me a currant bun as well and as I cycled back home I wouldn't have changed my lot with anyone.

I can still remember that Napier, dark green with black top and wings, brass radiator with a tall filler neck and huge brass acetylene headlamps. The engine was a big 6-cylinder, dead quiet and as smooth as silk. We never exceeded 34 mph, although the chauffeur assured me it would reach 40 if pushed.

My motoring was confined to these trips for a long time, but I kept up with it all through the motoring press. At that time there was an excellent weekly called *Auto*. It was only twopence, the same price as *Tiger Tim's Weekly* and *Rainbow*, so I gave them up and bought *Auto* instead. *The Autocar* and *Motor* were fourpence and beyond my reach, but the village garage was on my paper round and the proprietor took both of them. I remember thinking he must be very wealthy to have them both and used to wonder why he drove an 11.9 hp Bean instead of a Rolls Royce. On Tuesday mornings I used to start my round early and sit on a wall reading his *Motor* from cover to cover before popping it through his letterbox. On Fridays I repeated the performance with *The Autocar*.

In 1928 I left school and was apprenticed to a garage in nearby Walton. I had seen this place many times when out cycling and always stopped to look in the showroom. One day, acting on a sudden impulse, I went in, told them I was soon leaving school and asked for a job. The foreman looked me up and down, gave a bit of a grin and agreed to take me on. My parents were livid – they had got me down for the Civil Service – but nothing would change my mind.

In due course I reported for work. Naturally with all my reading I thought I knew it all and was most indignant when the foreman, instead of giving me a Bentley engine to overhaul, gave me a pile of filthy oily parts to clean! One of them was a huge undertray as fitted to a lot of cars in those days. This was off a 40 hp Fiat, a magnificent car belonging to a local bigwig with the unlikely name of Lady Clutterbuck. This tray ran from the radiator to behind the gearbox and, when stood on end, was about two foot taller than me. It was thickly coated with sticky gear oil, road dirt, dead flies etc and took me all day to clean. The foreman examined every inch of it before accepting it as clean, giving me an early lesson in 'If a job is worth doing it is worth doing well'. Most of the oil and muck was transferred to me and I got into big trouble when I got home.

I was put with an elderly mechanic of the old school. He was not very popular and I didn't like him much either, but he knew his job, taught me well and I never forgot the standards he set. In retrospect I owe him a lot.

I worked from 8 until 6 or later if a job had to go out and until 1 o'clock on Saturdays. My wages were 5/- (25p) a week, a pretty miserable wage even in those days, but I felt I was lucky to get paid at all for something I loved doing.

I soon progressed at my job. The mechanics were a pretty crude lot, using language I had never heard before and the younger ones' lurid tales of their exploits with women had me fascinated. However, they were good mechanics and, appreciating my keenness, taught me a great deal. We dealt with a good variety of cars and I recall working on Clyno, Calthorpe, Gwynne, Calcott and many other makes now long defunct.

American cars were also much in evidence and as 'puncture boy' I used to curse those wooden artillery wheels with their detachable split rims. I must confess that some of the previously unknown words picked up from the mechanics came in useful!

Our breakdown vehicle was a huge 1914 45 hp Renault, a fearsome beast with long flowing wings, large artillery wheels and a crane bolted on the back. The engine was a 4 cylinder in two blocks of two; the flywheel incorporated the fan and the gear lever worked in a quadrant instead of the usual gate. It took a strong man to start it on the handle which was the only means of doing so. It departed long before I could drive. We also ran a bus service from the town to the station using a 4 cylinder Chevrolet and a Morris Commercial. These were later joined by a 6 cylinder Star which was also used for trips to the coast at weekends. This was a beautiful machine, long and low, and would seat 28 people. It was before the days when coaches had the driver alongside the engine. He sat with the passengers behind a long bonnet flanked by flowing wings, just like a car. The model was aptly named by the makers the Star Flyer and it certainly did go, but unfortunately was not as robust as it should have been, persistent troubles being big-end failure and rear axle shafts. Soon after we got it a small company started up with three of them running a regular scheduled service from Weybridge to London. We got the contract to maintain them. They gave the same sort of troubles as our own so the workshops were usually graced with at least one Star Flyer. I made friends with one of the drivers, a long lanky fellow called Tom, and he often took me with him in the evenings or at weekends. He was a superb driver, sitting there with his peaked cap on the back of his head he would glide through the London traffic as if it wasn't there.

The venture was successful so of course it didn't take long for big business to cash in on their pioneering efforts and Green Line started a rival service. With their greater number of coaches and bigger organisation they were able to offer a more frequent and more reliable service and the Star operator closed down. I often wonder if any of these Flyers survived.

They were a happy bunch of mechanics, many practical jokes were played and, as the youngest and most naive, I was frequently the subject of them. I was once sent to the stores to get a long rest. The storekeeper, po-faced, sent me to one of the mechanics who, equally po-faced, sent me to another one. This went on until I had seen them all, so in desperation I asked the foreman. In very pithy terms he informed me that unless I got back to work I would get an even longer rest and at last the penny dropped!

I had my own back on the instigator. We had an ex-aeroplane starting magneto as a plug tester fitted with a handle which was turned to generate the H/T current. I set this thing up on the end of the bench, attached the live lead to a file and then laid a trail of metal bits to this fellow's vice. When he went to it I turned the handle as fast as I could and he leapt about four feet into the air.

In spite of the jolly atmosphere strict discipline was maintained. The foreman ruled with an iron hand. I called him Mister and the Manager Sir. I saw nothing wrong in this, it taught me to respect my elders and a bit more of that today wouldn't do any harm. The Directors were good types too. The MD was called 'Stodge' by his friends, I never knew why. The General Manager got himself the nickname 'Daisy' because he walked around humming, "Daisy, Daisy, give me your answer do". We approved of this as we always knew when he was coming!

Of course, more than anything I wanted to drive and watched the mechanics avidly when out on test with them. One day I was working next to a Calthorpe and the General Manager called out, "Ginger, bring that Calthorpe round to the front for me". It was obvious he did not realise I had never driven a car and I certainly was not going to tell him, so I jumped in, started it and drove round to the front, even managing a gear change. After this episode it seemed to be accepted that I could drive cars around the works and no excuse was too small to go a few yards. No more did I sweep under cars when cleaning up, I drove them, back, swept up and then drove them forward again.

One day a mechanic, bolder than the rest, let me take the wheel when out on test. The car was a bull nose Morris Cowley and I've had a soft spot for them ever since. My gratitude to him knew no bounds and, as making the tea was one of my more technical jobs, I rewarded him with my highest honour. For a whole week he had the first cup out of the pot and two spoons of sugar. Once more the incident seemed to start something and it became a normal thing for the mechanics to let young Ginger have a go when out on test. I was still only 15.

There were many fine cars in those days and we seemed to handle most of them. Walton was a wealthy district with lots of big houses; most of them had a big car and a smaller one, usually with a chauffeur. The latter were well looked after which resulted in a steady influx of work on high quality vehicles. In addition the Directors liked good cars, making trips to London to buy them for resale. As a result I was able to work on, and sometimes drive, such cars as Sunbeams, Delage, Bentley, Isotta-Fraschini as well as the more mundane Morris, Austin, Clyno, etc. We were agents for Austin and Morris so they formed the bulk of the everyday type of vehicle.

The various Sunbeam models were favourites of mine. I loved their beautifully finished engines and their impeccable behaviour on the road, the right hand gearchange being an absolute joy to use. Another lovely car to drive was the 14/45 Talbot, although the mechanics used to curse the small nuts and inaccessibility of the various components.

I was also involved, to some extent, with American cars. The MD, a portly man, liked them for their comfort, whilst their big woolly engines gave a good top gear performance and long periods without attention. Probably no other cars have gone through so many variations in style over the years as the big Yanks. They have, in fact, turned full circle from the classic lines of the late twenties and early thirties, the bulbous shapes of the late thirties and early forties, the grotesque horrors of the fifties to the acceptable shapes of the present day.

For a time he ran a Willys Knight 6-cylinder sleeve valve, a nice car but a bit of an oil burner. This was followed by a Falcon Knight, a smaller and cheaper version. I remember helping a mechanic to reline the brakes on this car. In those days there were no replacement shoes, we had our lining in a big roll, cut it to size, drilled and countersunk the rivet holes and invariably had to file it down because it was too thick. This car had both internal expanding and external contracting shoes on the rear. When relined there was very little clearance between the two so I had the job of filing them down so that we could get the drums on. It took me two whole days and my shoulder ached for weeks. With all the present day carry on about the dangers of asbestos dust I shudder to think how much I inhaled in those days.

One of the nicest of the American cars was the Chrysler. We saw very little of them because there was a distributor in neighbouring Weybridge, but in 1929-30 they brought out a cheaper version, the De Soto, and we became agents for them. They were very good cars, fast, quiet, very stylish and wonderful value for money. The MD had a two door version which was also used as a demonstrator and it gave no trouble at all. We were next door to a large film studio and most of the staff and visiting actors dealt with us. The De Soto appealed to the minor actors and directors who had little money but wanted an impressive car for their image.

One chap had a white roadster. After a month he decided he wanted it in red so we painted it in bright red with black wings. It looked superb but his wife didn't like it so we had to paint it white again. He was always boasting about his car and I suppose his colleagues got a bit fed up, for one day he came in with a terrible smell. We found some joker had tied a kipper to his silencer and I can still remember the glee with which the foreman wrote out the job card, "Remove kipper from exhaust system." There are no prizes for guessing who got the job of removing it!

We had other Yanks in as well, a lot of them from the studio, Marmon, Essex and Studebaker being fairly well represented.

All this time I was growing up and being taught other things as well as repairing motor cars.

I recall a lady with an Austin 12 fabric saloon which was constantly blowing exhaust flange gaskets. She had a very beautiful daughter and they both used to sit in the car whilst the gasket was changed. I could not understand why this car should require so many gaskets or why there was such competition amongst the mechanics to do the job. One day I found out.

The flange on these cars was at the back end of the manifold adjacent to the floor. Like most cars of the period the floorboards were removable and the easiest way to undo the back bolt was to take out one of the boards. Having done this the mechanic would poke his head under the bonnet to undo the other one and could look through the gap in the floor right up the skirt of the beautiful daughter. The reason the gasket kept blowing was because they deliberately left the nuts a bit loose. I had a feeling the girl guessed what was going on, but I'm sure mother never realised how much her daughter's short skirts and lovely legs were costing her in exhaust gaskets. Alas, by the time I was qualified to do the job she had bought another car!

I remember a very nice Austro Daimler that was bought for one of the Directors to use on his holiday in Scotland. One of the mechanics was detailed to check it over and when he came to the tappets he found that the clearance specified in English measurements was 0.040 in. He just couldn't believe it, almost every car in those days was either 0.004 in or 0.006 in and he was convinced it was a mistake so he set them all at 0.004 in. Next day a very irate Director rang up from Peterborough to say all the valves had burnt out.

We also had two Brocklebanks, another unusual car, both saloons and finished in brown with black wings and top. Although English they were very American in appearance and specification. They were smooth-running cars but lacked any sort of performance in spite of their 6-cylinder ohv engines. The brakes were hydraulic and outstanding; I feel they must have been one of the first British cars to be fitted with hydraulic brakes although Triumph had them about the same time.

Reliability was poor, clutches and rear axle shafts being two of their constant failures. I also recall an Ascot saloon, a sleeve valve 6-cylinder Imperia and a Waverley, all makes one never hears of today.

All sorts of tricks were performed in those days which would land you in trouble today and the foreman seemed to know them all. I recounted in a 'Motor Sport' article years ago the story of a 1923 Calcott which could not be induced to exceed 35 mph and a prospective purchaser didn't want to know. So, as the speedometer was driven by a belt from a pulley on the propeller shaft, a bigger pulley was made up. The speedometer then recorded 46 mph so the fellow bought it!

Another crafty operation was performed on the early Morris Minors. Their ohc engines gave them a very lively performance but they rapidly developed bore wear if given too much stick. The result, apart from increased oil consumption, was very noticeable piston slap. This put people off buying them secondhand, so instead of giving them an expensive rebore the pistons were withdrawn, oversize rings fitted and the skirts were squeezed in the vice to make them as oval as the bores! It worked too, all the noise disappeared and as far as I know none of the engines gave any trouble as a result.

I suppose these sort of things were all wrong but they didn't affect safety, caused nobody any harm and were more or less typical of the carefree spirit prevailing in those days.

2
THE EARLY DRIVING DAYS

I was now approaching seventeen and had already applied for my licence. It came through on my birthday (I still have it) and at last I was able to drive legally.

The foreman was only too pleased to send me out rather than an expensive mechanic, so I soon accumulated a lot of experience. Most of my driving was confined to the works hack. This was a 16 hp Daimler saloon, much too good for the job really, very upright with a vee windscreen. It wasn't much of a performer, being too heavy for its engine size and, like all sleeve valve engines, it used a lot of oil. The steering was very direct and the narrow tyres made it an absolute pig on wet tram lines. I took it under my wing keeping it clean, greased and oiled. My proudest moment was when I took it home to show my parents I really could drive, and a Daimler too, like the King used.

My driving was all fairly local and my first long run was in a flat nose Morris Cowley. The foreman was going to Southsea for his holiday and borrowed the car for the journey. I went with him to bring it back. Our local Scout troop was camping near Bognor so as soon as I was out of his sight I took the coast road and called in to see them, giving them all rides round the field.

I arrived home feeling very pleased with myself, so, fired with enthusiasm, hired a Morris Oxford to take my sister and her fiancé on a trip to Margate, picking up a girl friend who lived in London on the way.

This trip was a disaster! The car was terrible, hardly any brakes, dodgy steering and it overheated. Arriving in Margate a tram stopped quicker than I could. I couldn't get round it so had to hit it.

Damage was slight and the tram was unmarked, but my sister's day was ruined through worrying about the journey home. We managed it without hitting anything but the car boiled all the way, necessitating constant stops for water; and I was stopped by the police on Rochester Way who were suspicious of the way the car weaved about.

It was a long time before my sister came out with me again. The girl friend couldn't have been too impressed either as that was the last I saw of her.

The Daimler was replaced by a 1919 Bianchi tourer, a grand beast in bright yellow. All the fittings – radiator, lamps, etc. – were in brass, the gearchange needed two hands and the pedals needed two feet. The engine was a big 4-cylinder of around 26 hp. It was very high geared and loped along with an effortless gait. Stopping it was a different matter with only rear wheel brakes which were usually full of gear oil, hub oil seals in those days being just a ring of felt relying more on hope than anything else. I once came down Esher Hill with the near side tyres rubbing the kerb the whole way to help slow me enough for the bend at the bottom. It had other tricks like engaging two gears at once and backfiring into the carburettor, setting it alight. I carried a long tyre lever to deal with the former and a heavy wet cloth to put out the fire. It was a grand towing vehicle as it would pull anything and I frightened more people on the other end of the rope than I care to recall!

My everyday driving was not confined to the works hack. There were plenty of cars around, belonging to customers and Sales, and I never missed an opportunity to drive them. Many of them were good quality family cars that appealed to people who wanted, and could afford, something a bit more upmarket than the popular Morris and Austin.

It is customary nowadays to complain that the family type cars are practically all the same, but it wasn't all that different then. They were nearly all 4 cylinder side valve around 14 hp, available in open tourer or saloon form with artillery wheels. They did have distinctive radiators and, as the bonnet line had to be tailored to suit the front end, that at least gave them a bit of individuality. Four cars I find easy to recall: Bean, Crossley, Vauxhall and Hillman.

The Bean was a handsome open tourer finished in primrose yellow with black wings. We had it for some time. Whether it was a sales car they couldn't sell or was kept for some other reason I never knew, but it was always around and, although not actually used as a hack, if anyone had to go somewhere and their usual vehicle was not available they used the Bean.

I enjoyed driving it. Its performance wasn't bad, it felt very solid and well made, steering and brakes were good, so I was sorry when it eventually disappeared. It is the only Bean I have ever driven and if they were all as good as that one it is a great pity they ceased production.

The Crossley was a 14 hp open two seater belonging to a local businessman. There was nothing outstanding about it; like all Crossley it was well made but there was a very ordinary feel about it. I remember helping a mechanic reline the cone clutch. There was a very powerful spiral spring in the centre and I had to make up some long draw bolts to release the tension gradually thus preventing a possible embarrassing injury to the mechanic crouched in the cockpit.

The 14/40 Vauxhall was a nice enough car but rather stodgy and I thought it basked in the reflected glory of the illustrious 30/98. I was not destined to drive one of the latter until after the war when it had become 'Vintage'.

To revert back to Crossleys I did once drive a 19.6. Now that was a motor car!

The Hillman 14 was probably the best of the lot, although not the most expensive. It was lively, quiet, very smooth for a 4-cylinder and the right hand gearchange was first class. It was a much better car than the 6 cylinder Hillman Wizard that succeeded it. There was also a Hillman Straight Eight. We only had one of these and I seem to recall it gave a fair bit of trouble but it was a good car to drive.

Two very nice cars were the Segrave fabric bodied Sportsman's Coupé on the 14 chassis and a close coupled sports saloon on the Straight Eight. Both were designed by Sir Henry Segrave for his own use but were put into production as catalogue models. Segrave was one of my boyhood idols. Was that why I liked his Hillmans?

The various Humbers were good cars but not very inspiring until the arrival, in about 1929, of the 16/50 and Snipe. The original Snipe with right hand gearchange was a cracking car but I thought it lost a lot of character when, around 1930-31, they gave it a central gearchange and enclosed the wheel nuts in what I think were called Magnum wheels. Nevertheless they were still good cars.

A customer had a four light saloon with a fabric top and, I believe, dummy hood irons. He was an elderly man and frequently wanted to be driven, so hired me for the job. I got to like that car, especially when I had dropped him off somewhere and could give it a bit of stick on the way home.

It was an absolute tragedy when Humber, having joined up with Hillman, scrapped that lovely oh inlet, side exhaust engine and fitted the woolly old side valve unit from the bigger Hillman. Of course, it was not such a terrible thing as when the Rootes Group did the same thing to Georges Roesch's magnificent Talbots that was pure sacrilege.

The Morris Oxford had become a 6-cylinder by 1930, a very nice car with hydraulic brakes and a high standard of interior furnishing. The engine was still a side valve but had a metal cover over the head giving it the appearance of an ohv unit. In fact it was an early type of air filter, fumes being drawn up through ducts in the head and block, passing through some gauze before being sucked into the carburettor.

There were four body styles: an open tourer, fabric saloon, coachbuilt saloon and a very attractive close coupled coupé. They were popular and as Morris agents we sold a lot of them. I haven't seen one for years, but surely some of them have survived. A similar engine was put in the Morris Cowley and called the Morris Major, the good power/weight ratio gave it a sparkling performance. It was good fun to drive as it looked like an ordinary Cowley and people got quite a shock when you shot past them.

There was also a Morris Six, basically a Wolseley with a Morris radiator and a few other alterations. I have a feeling the Wolseley had four speeds and the Morris three, but could be wrong after all these years. We had a two seater coupé finished in grey with dark blue top and wings. I was once sent to collect it from that hub of London's motor trade, Warren Street. I loved going there, showrooms all the way along, cars for sale at the kerbside – imagine that now! Every conceivable make of second-hand car was represented.

Some of the traders were right villains but the atmosphere was terrific. On this occasion I was in a hurry to get back as I was meeting a smashing girl I had been trying to date for some time. Not knowing London very well in those days, I got well and truly lost, arriving home far too late. Ample compensation was provided by my drive in the Morris Six; after all, there were plenty of girls about but not many Morris Sixes!

The Wolseley was another make we saw a lot of. I recall with pleasure a 1926 ohc 10 hp two seater, a sturdy, well made little car and vaguely recollect an air cooled, horizontally opposed twin. The company was purchased by William Morris around 1927 and from then on the two makes had several common features.

The first Hornet was a little corker. Literally two cylinders added to the ohc Morris Minor, using the same body and a slightly longer chassis with hydraulic brakes, it went like a ding bat. It suffered from all the Minor's shortcomings and wore out very quickly, but until it did it was great fun. Encouraged by the Hornet the makers produced a bigger version, the Wolseley Viper. It was a dreadful car and didn't remain in production long. The mainstay of the Wolseley range was the "Silent Six". The kindest thing one can say about the joker who gave it that name is that hearing aids were not available as easily as they are today! It was a nice car to drive but certainly not silent.

What I did like was the Straight Eight. We had two regularly coming into the works. One belonged to the boss of a local furniture store and the other was owned by Castleton Knight, a well known film producer or director (I never know the difference). They weren't good cars really, but I thought them grand machines to drive. Progress along the road could only be described as majestic, like being on the bridge of a liner. I saw one advertised not all that long ago and was sorely tempted.

A well known barrister, later to become an Old Bailey judge, lived in the village. He was a charming man with great interest in the local community and one of his activities was to assist in the running of a club for the village teenagers. We played games like table tennis, held dances, put on sewing classes for the girls – all very similar to the Youth Clubs of today, only we didn't get drunk and smash the place up!

Through this club I got to known him well and persuaded him to deal with our garage. He had a Darracq, a nice car with black fabric body and red wheels. Performance was very good, but its biggest attribute was the exceptionally light, precise steering. The suspension and steering were perfectly orthodox, no different to our own cars to look at and I used to wonder how the French could get it so right.

We later sold him a Wolseley 21/60 'County' saloon. This was one of a new range of Wolseleys, a big improvement with a chain driven camshaft instead of skew gears and handsome, more roomy coachwork. The 'County' was the top of the range with every luxury available at that time, including a matching umbrella in a stand fixed to the o/s door pillar. Our barrister friend was very pleased with his and it gave him good service. Two other cars we became agents for were Swift and AJS. The Swift was well established as a rugged, reliable car, nothing spectacular but the sort of thing we made better than any other country. We took them on at the time they changed from the well known radiator shape to the thin shell type which was coming into fashion. At the same time they introduced their 8 hp model, the Swift Cadet. This was a nice little car, more roomy, better looking and better made than the contemporary Morris Minor, Austin 7, etc. It was a pleasant car to drive and deserved better success than it achieved.

The AJS was an attempt by the famous motor cycle manufacturers to enter the car market. It had a 10 hp side valve engine, most of them had fabric saloon bodies although other types were available. They were good little cars but did not have enough advantages over their rivals to justify the higher price so they too failed to weather the storm.

Another car I was fond of was the 2 litre Lagonda. We saw very little of them as the factory was only a few miles away and most local owners took their cars back there for service and repair. We had one or two on our books, mostly 14/60s and I loved both driving and working on them. The engine was a lovely piece of work, 4-cylinder with twin camshafts mounted high in the block operating the overhead valves, which were set at 90° in the beautifully machined combustion chambers. The whole chassis, engine, steering, brakes and suspension was built to an exceptionally high standard and the only drawback with it was that it was far too heavy to give a really brisk performance. Nevertheless, it was a delightful car to drive with a cruising speed very near its maximum and impeccable road behaviour.

One 14/60 open tourer belonged to a local ex-army officer, well known in the village. His driver was a Special Constable, later joining the Force full time. He retired many years ago and now works for the local Golf Club. We are still good friends and until I gave up my garage earlier in the year he was a regular customer. We often talked about the old days and about the old Lagonda we had both enjoyed over fifty years ago.

I recall another 14/60 which came in with a big-end gone and was found to require a crank grind.

Now Bill Smith, the foreman, was as good a mechanic as they come but he wasn't always right and his big failing was that he would never admit he was wrong. On this occasion he decided we could remove the crankshaft without taking the engine out. No one else thought much of this idea but he was the boss so work commenced. Before long it was obvious that although it might be possible it would be far easier to remove the unit and dismantle it in the normal way, but Bill was determined to prove his point. Eventually, after many hours of sweat and toil and to the accompaniment of the most dreadful language, the crank was removed. Re-assembling was another matter so after all that drama the engine had to be removed for the purpose of putting it all together again!

The owner of this car subsequently replaced it with a high chassis speed model, fitted with a Weymann fabric two door coupé body. This was a much livelier car, with extra power from the engine and a reduction in weight and its performance, although not startling, was much improved.

This type of two door fabric covered coupé body was quite popular at the time and very attractive. I think the Segrave Hillman was the first one to be called a Sportsman's Coupé but other manufacturers, notably Rover, were quick to follow suit and the 'sportsman' soon had a choice. The styling with two wide doors, covered-in rear quarters and a large trunk at the back was clean and businesslike. The rear seat was really only for occasional use but all the passengers sat within the wheelbase. I suppose one could say they were the original 2+2s. The 16 hp Rover version was a very good car and extremely nice to drive.

It is many years since I have seen any of these late Twenties or early Thirties 6-cylinder Rovers. Two models were made, 16 hp and 20 hp. They were good sturdy, well-made cars and I would have thought some might have survived. I suppose it could be that most of them had fabric bodies which have rotted away over the years. One that particularly appealed to me was a two door close coupled fabric saloon with cycle type front wings that turned with the wheels. I think it was called the 'Blue Train', had the

16 hp engine and was a nice car to drive. Like most cars of the period the Rover had simple but pleasing lines, uncluttered with emblems and badges proclaiming this and that to people who are not really interested. I have to confess that when sitting at the lights I cannot get terribly worked up because the car in front has fuel injection, 5 speeds, a 1.8 litre engine and various other features which are no doubt important to the owner.

Looking back I would say that very few innovations have had such a far reaching effect on the appearance of cars as chromium plating. Can you imagine a modern car with all the moulding and other embellishments in nickel or brass? Yet up to about the end of 1929, a bit earlier with the Yanks, all the plated parts had to be cleaned with metal polish.

Fortunately it was not part of my job to clean cars but occasionally, if the cleaner was off sick or something, I had to do it. The radiator, lamps and bumpers if fitted – not many cars had them then – were not too bad, but I hated the fiddly bits like windscreen frames and door handles.

Worst of all were the wheel nuts. The Morris Cowley had three per wheel, the Oxford had five, so given a choice I always cleaned a Cowley. There were still cars about with nickel plating up to the beginning of the war. After all, a 1928 car was then only eleven years old and there are plenty of 1975 cars about today.

Eventually the stout-hearted old Bianchi joined the Daimler in the local breaker's yard and was replaced by a 1927 Morris Oxford tourer. This had four wheel brakes and displayed a red triangle on the back to warn following drivers to keep their distance. It was, in fact, an early example of what is now known as 'bull' because it didn't stop much better than the old Bianchi. Still it did make people keep further back, although had they known it they would have been in much more danger in front. The trouble with Morris brakes of the period lay in the compensators. These took the form of a sprocket either side of a cross shaft with a chain connected to the rods. After all these years I forget the exact layout but the theory was that the chain only moved over the sprocket enough to actuate the brakes so they remained even. What really happened was the whole mechanism got covered in water and dirt from the road and seized up. They were marvellous cars, those old Oxfords, taking all sorts of punishment and coming up for more, their only weakness being rear axle shafts.

We had great service out of this one until one day we had a chassis frame going to a firm in South London to be straightened after an accident. One of the junior salesmen knew where the place was and offered to take it, placed in the back of the Oxford and sticking out over the windscreen. Within a mile that unfortunate chassis frame was involved in another accident. I never really knew what happened but our faithful old Morris was a write off, resulting in it joining the others in the breaker's yard. Just before this we got the agency for Dodge. These were really Chryslers with a different radiator, an early example of badge engineering. We had a Straight Eight roadster as a demonstrator, very beautiful in pale grey with green wings, green upholstery and wire wheels. This was a really super car and was the fastest I had driven.

Whilst we were dealing with Dodge there was a week-long agricultural show in nearby Chertsey and the factory loaned us a few trucks to exhibit. As the show was on open ground they were brought back each night and I managed to get in on the daily trip.

My vehicle was a 30 cwt truck, a 6-cylinder, very smooth and fast with a cabin nearly as good as a car. It made the contemporary Morris Commercial which we also handled, seem very primitive.

Another American car I drove at the same time was an old Studebaker, about 1926-7, belonging to a local dentist. This was a big square vehicle which felt like a small lorry. Instead of an accelerator pedal the throttle was operated by a ball set in a cup on the floorboards. As you put your foot down the ball swivelled, giving a delightfully smooth action.

Unfortunately the cup used to trap all the dirt with the result that the throttle would stay open. This led to some very dodgy moments; you couldn't get your foot under it to bring it back so the only thing to do was to switch off, slip into neutral and apply the brakes. As the brakes were operated via an early example of engine driven servo, this didn't help much either.

Our Morris Oxford had been replaced by an Austin 12 tourer of 1928 vintage, a very solid car ideal for the job except that towing anything heavy tended to make the clutch slip.

A large proportion of cars in those days were open, traffic was light and most journeys were a pleasant experience with none of the aggro of the present day. In towns trams were a bit of a hazard but one got used to them, particularly their stopping power which was far superior to the average car. The tramlines were also a bit of a menace when it was wet, tyres had not the grip of present day radials and were much narrower. It was easy for a cyclist to get a wheel in one and fall off so one had to watch them very carefully.

There were no motorways, very few dual carriageways, no parking restrictions or traffic wardens, and for the first year or so of my driving, no mobile police. It caused quite a commotion when the first traffic patrols started. Around these parts they used Morris Cowley two seaters, Jowetts and later Hillman Wizards. Later on they got Humber 16s and Wolseley 18/85s. Most of these were saloons with a rear window blind that had 'Stop, Police' written on it. They would nip in front of their victim and pull the blind up and the story goes that one day the miscreant pulled out, nipped in front of the police car pulling up his blind which read 'Get Lost, Bandits'!

The standard of driving was higher too as people were not in such a hurry. Also there was more skill attached to driving with crash gearboxes, indifferent brakes and none of the present day aids to comfort. I think most people having mastered something difficult take a pride in doing it and in the case of motoring they drove accordingly.

In the early thirties our garage changed hands. The mass-produced car was taking over and such stalwarts as Swift, Clyno, Calthorpe, etc., were replaced with Ford 8s, Morris 10s, Hillman Minxes and the like. Our guv'nor, like many of his contemporaries, went to the wall. We were purchased by a Ford Main Dealer from London and I was sold with the business like a slave of old.

We naturally became more involved with Fords but continued with other makes. Cars were getting more sophisticated, being mostly saloons with synchromesh gearboxes and other mod cons. One bright spot was the influx of the mass-produced small sports car. The MG Midget and Magna, Wolseley Hornet Special, Singer Le Mans, all brought fun motoring to people who could not afford cars like Aston Martin and Lagonda and I was fortunate enough to get well involved with these.

I've always had a liking for six cylinders so my favourites were the 6-cylinder MG Magna and the Hornet Special. Of the two the Magna was the better built and had a race bred chassis but the Hornet was a better proposition, having very good hydraulic brakes, a chain driven camshaft which was quieter and less trouble than the MG's drive through the dynamo and a greater variety of body styles. Both rapidly became oil burners and the Hornet was a bit inclined to big end failure, but they were great fun to drive. Had I been in the position to buy one it would have been the MG; having seen their exploits at Brooklands and read about them elsewhere I was a bit of an MG fan.

One day I was sent up to London to collect the MD's new Ford. It looked like a standard Model B saloon, a 4-cylinder side valve car, very rugged but not noted for its performance. As I started it I realised it was no ordinary Model B. It was quiet, smooth and felt quite different. I nosed out into the traffic, saw a gap and put my foot down. The effect was devastating. The rear wheels spun leaving thick black marks on the road, then they gripped and the car shot forward like a rocket, streaking up the road in a manner that was quite out of this world in 1933. As soon as possible I pulled into a side road to see what I was driving, lifted the bonnet and found a big hulk of V8. It turned out to be one of a batch handed out to main dealers before being announced to the public which was the reason I hadn't heard of it. It was, in fact, a standard Model B with a V8 engine and its performance was terrific as well as being smooth and quiet. Unfortunately, the steering and brakes were quite inadequate for the performance of the engine; they weren't much good with the 4-cylinder engine but the V8 put the cars into the 'very dicey' category.

An amusing incident occurred with this car. The MD came down one day to have lunch with our manager. He complained of a lumpy tick over, said none of his chaps in London could tune it and had we got anyone? For some reason the manager put me on to it. I knew nothing about V8 engines and the carburettor was strange to me but, probably more by luck than anything else, I found the trouble and got it ticking over like a watch. They went off for lunch, had a good two hour session and came out to find the engine still quietly ticking over. I had got it so smooth he had forgotten to switch it off! He was tickled pink and after that I got all the V8's to tune.

One car I was particularly fond of was the Invicta, a wonderful car to drive, especially the low chassis 100 mph model. I never drove one at a hundred but did manage ninety on one occasion, the fastest I had driven and my new 'speed record'. These cars were beautifully made and the chassis was a work of art, only the finest materials being used and the workmanship was superb. I seem to remember that the frame was of chrome nickel steel and wherever possible phosphor bronze was used for the various fittings.

Meadows supplied the engines but each one was stripped at the Invicta works and carefully rebuilt by their own mechanics. They had something of a reputation for being twitchy at high speeds but I always doubted if it was justified.

Raymond Mays performed incredible feats with his but, of course, he was a driver of immense skill. On the other hand the great, incomparable Sammy Davis had a monumental accident in one at Brooklands although he was careful to point out in one of his books that it was no fault of the car. Nevertheless, many years later when I had the great privilege of getting to know him, he did hint once that although the car was not to blame for the accident it might have been less serious had he been driving something else.

Be that as it may, they were fantastic motor cars, there was nothing else I would sooner have had and I still feel the same way. There is no doubt that if one day that elusive big pools win comes my way I will look for a low chassis 'S' Type Invicta and will buy it if it means spending the lot. Another favourite car was a Stutz owned by a local resident. The straight eight ohc engine was more continental in design than American and the car was a treat both to drive and to work on. It would do everything in top gear but if you felt like it a bit of fun and used the gears it would out perform almost anything. I remember one of them giving the Bentleys a fright in the Le Mans 24 hour race, and Bentley enthusiast that I am, I was secretly very pleased when it came in second.

It was the policy of most American manufacturers at the time to market a smaller and cheaper car alongside their main product. I have mentioned the Falcon Knight and De Soto from Willys and Chrysler respectively, but there was also the Erskine from Studebaker, Marquette from Buick, Essex from Hudson and La Salle from Cadillac. These were not necessarily smaller and cheaper versions of their parent cars, although they naturally shared some common features, but separate makes in their own right.

One I particularly liked was the Erskine, a middle size 6-cylinder Saloon of around 17 hp, very lively with a fair turn of speed, quiet and comfortable. Two Marmon straight eights were also regular visitors, a saloon and a two seater roadster. They were excellent cars, probably one of the best Yanks of their day apart from the very expensive and prestige vehicles like Duesenberg, Stutz and Packard. Towards the end of their manufacturing life Marmon made a magnificent car with a light alloy engine, either a V12 or a V16, I forget which after all these years. I saw one at Olympia in the early Thirties but never saw one on the road.

As I was now starting to earn a bit more money I got myself a motor bike. It was a 1929 250 sv BSA, not very exciting but a good little bike and one of the first to have a saddle tank. In spite of this up to date feature it still had acetylene lighting and my first job was to convert it to electric. I had a few adventures with that bike. One dark, wet Saturday evening I was on my way to pick up a girlfriend to take her to the village hop. Unbeknown to me there was an Indian motorcycle combination behind me. He too had an acetylene lamp which was pretty well on its last legs. The street was badly lit and I was wearing black; he didn't see me put my arm out to turn right, suddenly realised I was doing so and did a violent swerve

The dyed-in-the-wool vintage motorcycle enthusiast goes for the traditional "flat-tanker". In 1928 however most British manufacturers adopted the now universal saddle tank arrangement which can be seen on my first road going machine, this 1928 250 sidevalve BSA. It cost me a hard earned £3 and of course in those days we never wasted time with crash hats which were for serious racing men or "pansies". The acetylene head lamp went out everytime I hit a bump and was eventually fitted with a 6 volt bulb conversion. One way or the other I managed to provide illumination but didn't have too many regrets when I eventually sold the machine for a handsome profit at £4

straight into the village baker's shop.

He turned out to be the drummer in the band playing at the hop, with all his kit in the sidecar. He was quite unhurt, we had the usual argument about whose fault it was but it was all quite friendly and between us we pulled his machine out of the wrecked shop doorway. It was surprisingly free from damage and still driveable so he got on and carried on to the dance. I had a chat with him during the interval and we remained friends until he died about ten years ago. The baker wasn't all that happy about it but you can't please everybody!

It was about this time I became an insurance agent. My BSA was insured with the London and Lancashire and for reasons that escape me now they asked me to become their local agent. It seemed a good way to make some extra cash so I agreed. There was a lot of palaver, character references and that sort of thing but it came through and I set up shop.

Soon afterwards I sold the bike to a young lad who was on the fringe of our gang and proudly signed him up as my first client. It was Third Party only with a premium of a few shillings but it was a start.

All went well for about a month and then disaster struck. At the end of the High Street, just before it curved to join another road, was a farm. On the opposite side was a field used for cattle grazing and every afternoon old Sam Eagle the cowman would drive his cows across the road to the farm for milking. One afternoon young Ted came flying round the corner straight into them. He hit one cow, which let out a bellow of rage, lashed out and sent him flying into old Sam who went down with a broken leg. The other cows stampeded, panic stricken, up the High Street causing considerable havoc. The whole episode cost the insurance company a lot of money and as he was the only client I got them it was not surprising they suggested it might be better if I handed over the agency to someone else. I must have been the most expensive agent they ever had. Ted wisely decided that bike was getting a bit too well-known in the village and sold it.

Having the princely sum of £4 in my pocket from the sale of the BSA, I looked round for another bike. Before I found one a fellow came into the garage with a 1928 Morris Oxford coupé with a rear dickey seat. The clutch had gone, he couldn't afford a new one so I bought it for £3:5s. This left me with a surplus of fifteen shillings from the sale of the bike, so I was really chuffed. The car was taxed and insured so, having put a new clutch in it, I was on the road. I got fantastic service out of this car. Apart from my running about I used to hire it out to the lads for their snogging, 2/6 for the evening, 5/- on Saturdays. On Sundays I used it for my own snogging.

No car was ever run on a more slender shoestring. I tried to work it so that the tank was empty when one of the boys had it for the evening and there was always a little drop in it when it came back. All topping up of oil was done with oil drained out of customers' cars on the first services. I couldn't afford to buy tyres so used to save any in my size that were taken off other people's cars. Obviously they were not removed from someone else's car until they were worn out but if they hadn't got a hole in them they were good tyres as far as I was concerned. No MOT in those days.

Just as the tax and insurance were running out I sold it to a lady wanting a temporary car whilst hers was being repaired, making a small profit. Within three weeks she got her own car back and asked me to sell the Morris for her. It was now taxed and insured for another three months, so I made no attempt to sell it, carrying on as before until the tax ran out again. My old pal, the local breaker, then gave me about £3 for it. The dear lady was so pleased she gave me a pound back for my trouble. This was my first car – to date I have now owned 74 – and, bearing in mind the value of money in those days, it was probably my most profitable.

I had now got a few pounds saved up so bought an Austin 7 for £5:10s a 1926 Chummy. It was a bit scruffy but I got a tin of red paint and some black for the wings and set to. I soon found out it used more oil than petrol so another trip to the breaker was indicated, this time as a purchaser. He had a set of later type pistons slightly oversize, but as my bores were well worn it didn't take me long to machine them to fit. The bottom end was in good shape so I finished up with a nice little engine.

That little car gave me a lot of pleasure; often grossly overloaded with bods, it did thousands of miles. Once, when going to Leigh-on-Sea to visit relations, a rear spring broke on a particularly rough tramline junction in the East End of London. I wasn't too worried about the effect on the suspension, but it left the axle unlocated on that side which was a bit dodgy. I pulled into a side road, removed the broken bit and forced the shock absorber arm on to the spring locating pin on the axle. To my surprise this temporary expedient worked a treat and it remained like that until I got rid of it.

The works Austin 12 now joined all its predecessors and was replaced by a Ford Model B saloon. It was the 24 hp version which gave it a reasonable performance. It was very much a scaled up version of the Ford 8 and, like all the other Fords, the brakes were poor even by the standards of the day. One of the reasons was the design of the king pin assemblies; the slightest over-enthusiasm with the grease gun and the surplus grease got on to the linings, making a poor system even worse. One of the reasons the Morris 8 sold so well was its hydraulic brakes.

The garage then changed hands again, Ford and Citroën – which we had also taken up – were out and the new concern became agents for Triumph. The three new Directors had no previous experience of the motor trade. The MD had been a shipbuilder in Sunderland, but they were keen to learn and were very decent chaps, so we all worked hard to help them make a go of it. It was nice to work for a small company again and to have a better class of car to work on.

At that time I was doing a bit of mild tuning on Morris 8s. I have no recollection as to how this came about but I remember doing several of them. I would remove the head, machine a few thou. off the face, grind off all the rough bits and polish the combustion chambers. The head was then sent for copper plating. The ports were polished and matched up with the manifolds, valves polished, ground in and refitted with double springs. With this treatment they would stand a more advanced ignition setting and different carburettor needles. A straight-through Burgess exhaust would complete the job and the result, though not startling, certainly justified all the effort.

Our new MD had a Triumph Gloria open sports tourer, a nice car, well made with good steering and brakes but a bit too heavy to give a sporty performance. When he saw what I was up to with Morris 8s he got me to do it for him. His car had the 4-cylinder Coventry Climax engine with overhead inlet and side exhaust valves, a fairly robust engine but an unknown quantity as far as I was concerned. I was given a free hand and unlimited time so was able to be meticulous with the assembly and could pay great attention to detail. The results surprised me and delighted him so I got off to a good start with my new boss.

I thought the Triumphs were very good cars, well made and finished inside and out, a comprehensive instrument panel with large speedometer and rev. counter, nice leather upholstery with polished wood fascia and cappings. They were nowhere near as popular as they should have been, especially as their steering, road holding and brakes matched their looks. Around 1937 they brought out a new range with all ohv engines. These were both 4- and 6-cylinder, very rugged and with plenty of poke.

The body style being the same for both engines, they were distinguished only by the longer bonnet of the Six. I think this was the time when the name Vitesse came into the Triumph nomenclature and they were very good cars. Later on the Dolomite came into the picture, a handsome car with a futuristic front grille known as the waterfall. The saloon was complemented by a striking roadster and the 6-cylinder version had three carburettors. There were two other Directors, both younger than the MD, splendid fellows and fond of nice motor cars. One had a 20 hp SS1 open tourer which I will cover in the Jaguar chapter, the other had a Talbot 105 fitted with a sports coupé body by Van den Plas, a very smart machine in black with red interior. This car really did go and very few cars that came my way could match it on acceleration, possible exceptions being the Ford V8 and the Railton straight eight. It was fitted with the pre-selector gearbox which made lightning changes possible and this, coupled with the immense power developed by the engine, really got it off the mark. It was relatively trouble free and the only problem we ever had was violent wheel wobble at speed. It was really vicious and one could not drive through it. I cannot remember now what the trouble was, but I do remember it took a lot of finding and some very hairy high speed test runs were involved.

This fellow had a mother who was obviously no chicken, but liked sporty motor cars. Originally she had a Wolseley Hornet Special fitted with a very pretty coupé body by Eustace Watkins. It was similar in shape to the Salonette body fitted to the F-type MG Magna but was set off better by long flowing wings. She used to drive it flat out all the time and it became a full-time job keeping it in tune.

In due course the Hornet was replaced by a 1½-litre Frazer Nash-BMW sports saloon. I had never driven one and thought at first she had made a bad swop, but the first time I took it out I was captivated. What a cracking little car it was, fast, smooth, flexible and it handled like a dream.

About this time I handled one or two Astin Martins, the delightful 1½-litre International and Ulster models. These were beautiful cars to drive, thoroughbreds in every respect. The gear change was a bit tricky and acceleration wasn't their strong point, but they looked and felt just right. Meanwhile I had purchased a 1931 Austin 7 saloon, my best car to date, which cost me £28:10s. It was a cracking little car, dark blue and black, in very good shape both mechanically and bodily. I kept it for a very long time and recall taking it to Mumbles in South Wales for a holiday, the first of many visits.

My employer was not too keen on the idea of me risking life and limb on two wheels and pushed me into buying this little 1931 Austin Seven which was a pleasant relief after the series of highly unreliable mobile wrecks that preceded it. It cost me £28 which was a princely sum in those days. I managed to find a sizeable deposit and my boss helped me out by deducting 5/- (25p) per week from my wages. I got a great deal of pleasure from the Austin which had the benefit of a foot brake operating on all four wheels unlike the previous handbrake/foot brake division of labour. Although it had its limitations as a courting car I have many happy memories of it which were revived when I saw GH 2949 ahead of me on the road after the war when I was driving home from Goodwood.

One day after the war I was coming home from Goodwood and there in front of me was GH 2949, my old pride and joy. Traffic conditions did not permit me to stop so I was not able to have a chat with the owner. I sold it eventually to one of my pals and bought a 1933 BSA 10 hp saloon with a preselector gearbox and fluid flywheel. It was a nice looking little car, well made and very nice inside. The performance wasn't exciting but it was comfortable and would maintain a surprising average speed on a long run. I didn't keep it long as my brother-in-law happened to mention it to a colleague and it transpired he had been looking for a small preselector car for some time, having some problem that made normal gear changing difficult. After a certain amount of haggling he bought it and I took his 1934 Ford 8 in part exchange.

Around 1935 we got involved with a dynamic little man by the name of Bensusan who came to the area as South Eastern manager of a Cornish company making air compressors, pneumatic drills and similar equipment. He had a Wolseley Hornet in which he covered an astronomical mileage, all of it either flat out or towing a caravan, sometimes both. This unfortunate little car was only off the road for the few hours that he slept and stuck it in a manner which surprised everybody. He rented one of our offices and a corner of the workshop to set up a London Service Dept., being shortly joined by a young engineer from the factory complete with a brand new Austin 7 van.

He had spent very little time away from his native Cornwall and was a bit like a fish out of water, but he was a nice bloke so we took him into the fold. Unfortunately for us he was a good looking chap with a pleasant personality. It was not long before we realised he was grabbing a considerable share of the eligible crumpet and we suspected the back of his van was being used for purposes other than the transportation of pneumatic drills. Obviously we hadn't this in mind when we took him in but realising that jealousy would get us nowhere we accepted it as a fact of life.

Their Service Dept. was soon established and before long he had more work than he could cope with, so it was arranged that when a compressor came in for overhaul I would do the engine whilst he did the rest of it. These engines were my old friends, the Hotchkiss-type Morris Oxfords, so I felt at home. They usually wanted a rebore and new bearings; sometimes a crankshaft was worn when I would have it ground and bored in line, but usually they just needed new bearings which I scraped in by hand.

This soon led to me doing other things for them, overhauling the compressors, drills and other air tools; it made a change and was good experience.

Jack the engineer, like most Cornishmen, was rightly very proud of his County and one evening was boasting in the local about Cornish beer. On his next trip home he brought back a flagon but was daft enough to leave it in his van. With great care we steamed off the paper band sealing the screw top, drank the beer, refilled the bottle with water and re-sealed it. That evening he took it to the pub. "Right chaps", he said. "I'll show you a drop of real beer". The landlord produced some glasses, Jack poured out and couldn't believe his eyes "A bit pale, Jack", said the landlord and took a swig, ejecting it with great force as soon as he tasted it. Poor Jack was most put out but we never heard any more about Cornish beer. It became part of my job to tow the compressors back to their sites after overhaul, set them up and leave them running. Our Model B Ford was just the thing for this, having ample power, but the brakes were even less effective with a heavy machine on tow and I had quite a few dicey moments.

Going down the North Circular Road one day, the traffic came to a sudden stop. In front of me was a British Oxygen lorry which loomed nearer and nearer as I tried frantically to pull up. Just when I thought I must hit it the blockage cleared and the lorry moved off.

Another time I was taking a machine to Ascot. Descending the hill at Sunninghill I found a telephone engineer's van parked at the bottom. There was room to get through so I carried on but just then another telephone van came round the corner, the driver saw his mate and stopped opposite to have a chat.

With my finger on the horn button and lights flashing I bore down on them, the second driver got the message and shot forward leaving me just enough room. This compressed air work took me to some interesting places. I recall a glass bottle factory, a stone mason, a shoe factory and there were others, as well as construction sites. I usually found someone who would show me round and I learned quite a lot about other people's jobs.

The film studios previously mentioned were still there and continued to provide me with nice cars to drive. I expect most of my contemporaries remember Carl Brisson, a superb actor and singer. He was at the studios for a long time and had a magnificent Isotta-Fraschini. Everything on this car was massive. We once put a clutch in it and the gearbox was so big and heavy it required two men to lift it. The straight eight engine was a joy to behold, beautifully made and finished with no external pipes or wires to spoil the effect. On the road it was fast and flexible but a bit heavy, even by the standards of the day.

Carl Brisson was so fond of this car that when it got a bit tatty he had the chassis overhauled and a new body fitted by Lancefield. This was a more sporty saloon with a trunk on the back, painted throughout in white. If this car still exists it must be worth a fortune – it was beautiful. Other nice cars to come from the studios were a Delage D8 with a close coupled fabric body, several 3½-litre Bentleys, a Packard Straight 8 roadster, an Auburn Speedster, and a Cord. We did quite well out of it apart from the pleasure it gave me, but it wasn't always easy to get money out of some of these characters.

We had one fellow with a Chrysler straight eight roadster, a lovely car with wire wheels and twin sidemounts, and he came in regularly for small jobs which he paid for. One day he announced he wanted the car in tip top order for the winter and would we fit six new tyres, a new battery, new plugs and anything else required. He collected it at the end of the day, took the bill, saying he would drop in next day to pay it. That was the last that we ever saw of him. When he didn't come in I went round to the studios to remind him only to be told his film was finished, he was no longer there and no-one knew where to contact him. We were as upset as the boss. He was a thoroughly decent type and we were furious that he had been caught. Had we been able to find that scoundrel he would have had a pretty rough time.

On one occasion I was roped in for a film. It was a sort of bank robbery effort and involved the getaway car skidding into a ditch. I was supposed to come up with our old Morris Commercial breakdown crane, lift it out quickly and the villains would then jump in and drive off. It was stressed I had to be double quick and lift it out in one go so I practised for about two days. The big day came and it all went like clockwork. The Directors congratulated me and gave me a pound. I waited for weeks for the film to be shown at the local cinema and proudly took my current girlfriend to see it, only to find they had cut my bit out. So ended my film career.

Towards the end of 1936 we became agents for MG, just about the time they changed from ohc cable braked cars, originally conceived by Cecil Kimber, to the push rod ohv, hydraulic braked TA. To me they weren't the same but they were still a sports car and I had to admit were better on the road.

I went on a course to the factory in Abingdon and got really genned-up.

My speciality was still tuning and I gave several TAs the old Morris 8 treatment except for copper plating the head which by that time had gone out of fashion, as it were. It probably didn't do much good anyway. Results fully justified the time and effort and the cars performed much better for a relatively small outlay.

Another experiment, which was not a success, was supercharging the MD's 2-litre drophead. This was a very nice car which he bought with a low mileage and repainted it in silver grey with a pale grey mohair hood. We agreed to use it for experimental purposes at the request of the makers of Marshall superchargers situated in Hanworth, not very far away. There was much to be done not only in the fitting of it but in designing a new manifold,

Eventually I decided that a larger vehicle was essential for camping and courting and bought this 1933 Rover Ten for the purpose. Unlike the later models of its type it retained a separate iron block and aluminium crankcase. The general fragility of its bottom end with two bearing crankshaft regularly resulted in big end failure particularly when flat out with four up. It was in this car that I experienced my narrowest escape at the wheel including racing when on a narrow road near Neath I failed to observe a long steel girder projecting from the rear of a lorry approaching me which turned into a gateway leaving the girder at neck height across the road. We just stopped in time to avoid decapitation and were grateful for the hydraulic brakes which for some inexplicable reason were on later models changed for rod operated Girlings. The faithful Rover was used for ARP work during the early years of the war before changing hands

deciding on the right size and type of carburettor, working out pulley sizes etc. I took the car to them, removed the manifold and sundry other fittings, they took templates of the ports and flanges, we worked out how the blower could be fitted, throttle linkage, various other odd bits and then I put it back together.

In due course they informed us they were ready. I took the car back and we fitted up the new parts. Carburation had to be a bit of trial and error as no data was available, but having previously decided on an SU we made a guess at the required jet and needle size, pressed the starter button and to everyone's astonishment it burst into life. It obviously wasn't right so, having provided myself with a selection of jet needles, I fiddled about until it was at least a runner, returning then to the garage to continue on my own ground, so to speak.

I got it right in due course and the car went very well, but the improvement was insufficient to justify all the trouble and expense so the project was dropped. The big snag was the tendency of these cars to knock bearings out at the best of times, thus limiting the blower pressures to a figure below that required to give good results. However, it was an interesting experiment and a welcome change from routine.

I continued to swap my own cars. They were never very exciting but I got plenty of fun out of my job so opted for practical vehicles for my own use.

This sidevalve Morris Eighteen belonged to my boss but he lent it to me for occasions when I needed a really big car. Here it is seen on a holiday trip to Scotland during which we met a couple of charming young ladies with whom we became so involved on one occasion that we failed to notice that the handbrake had been knocked off during a moment of passion allowing the car to run back and almost over the cliff. The Morris was ideal for covering long distances in an effortless manner

The last one I had before the war was a Rover 10, not a startling performer but roomy and comfortable on a long run.

By this time Mumbles had become a favourite place to spend a week-end, the Gower peninsula was completely unspoiled with miles of beautiful coastline and charming little bays. Mumbles itself was a small coastal village with just enough commercial attractions to make it interesting, whilst Swansea was near enough it we wanted to go on the town. There were usually four of us and we would travel over Friday night, arriving in the small hours and pitch our tent on the cliff top. We would normally return on the Sunday night, but one Bank Holiday week-end we stayed until Monday, starting for home when The Mermaid turned out at 10.30. We got as far as Lydney and found a dance in progress. Apart from the local talent the bar was open until one o'clock so we stopped off and joined the fun. Having left about one, we were nearing

Gloucester when the Rover started to boil; a top hose had split. I bound it up with some tape and a handkerchief and an obliging local who was still up gave us some water and a milk bottle. There was still a hundred miles to go, the hose was not completely holding water, it was obvious we would need some more and the chances of getting it at that time of night were pretty remote.

Fortunately, between us we had drunk a considerable amount of beer and as the call of nature was roughly pro rata to the needs of the cooling system, we arrived home without further mishap.

I still had the Rover when war broke out. The garage was taken over by Vickers for the manufacture of parts for Wellington bombers. I went to Gloster Aircraft, later being transferred to Hawkers at Langley where I carried out final inspection of Hurricanes prior to their first test flight until I was able to join the RAF myself. During this period I had an Austin 10 but, as petrol got scarce, changed to an Austin 7 Ruby and finally to an Ariel Red Hunter motor bike.

The mid-Thirties had seen a gradual change from the old carefree motoring days and the rot was setting in; no more could you go where you liked, stop where you liked and, within the bounds of common sense, do what you liked. The war finished it off altogether and when we returned it was to a different world.

3
POST WAR YEARS TO THE EARLY FIFTIES

In spite of my gloomy predictions, early post-war motoring wasn't too bad within the mileage limits imposed by petrol rationing. I started off with another Ariel Red Hunter, a 500 cc single port and a jolly good bike.

While I was still away I received a letter from John Heath saying he had bought my old garage and, subject to a satisfactory interview, would like me to return as Service Manager. I had risen to be a foreman before the war and reckoned I could do the job, so joined him as soon as I could.

John was in partnership with George Abecassis but at first I saw little of him as he was running their little garage at the other end of the town. This was later sold and we all settled down to establish H W Motors. At first I only had one mechanic and a boy, so during the day I put on my overalls and carried out repairs, returning after supper to do my paper work. At weekends I operated the petrol pumps. I've no idea what I did in my spare time!

The mechanic died some years ago but the boy, now middle-aged with a family, works in a local garage I am friendly with and I often see him. We were soon joined by a Sales Manager, an old Etonian, extremely pleasant and willing to help out in any way. The secretary, Olive Vaughan, had also been there before the war and had more or less stayed around all the time; she also

There isn't much that you could say about the Morris Eight, which provided me with practical transportation despite an almost total lack of performance.

had to do everything in the office, even down to making the coffee. This then was the little team that got HWM off the ground.

Initially a lot of our work involved getting cars out of wartime storage and preparing them for use. I can remember some of them, a Packard Super 8, a Pontiac Straight Eight, the local MP's 3½-litre Bentley, a Hotchkiss and a straight eight Nash, rather a rare bird with a dual ignition system.

After being starved of motoring for so long it was a treat to drive such cars again but petrol rationing limited the amount I could use them. During this period I had the use of two cars. I had kept in touch with my old boss who, during the war, had been with the Ministry of Aircraft Production, liaising with Rolls Royce and De Havillands. He had bought an MG TB Tickford DHC for use as a second car to his 2-litre , and he was kind enough to lend it to me until I got sorted out.

This was a delightful little car with all the sporting characteristics of the open two seater coupled with saloon car comfort. I liked the TB although not many were built; it was similar to the TA except for the engine and gearbox which were based on the Morris 10 Series M. The later post war TC was almost the same, the main difference being that MG's had abandoned their long standing sliding trunnion mounting for the back end of the rear springs and were using ordinary shackles. There was no technical merit in the new arrangement so I suspect it was done to use more Morris 10 parts. I had a lot of fun with this car and would very much like one today.

The other car was a 1935 Morris Isis. It was a sort of spare car about the place registered as a taxi to get extra petrol coupons. I was able to use it when I required a larger car than the MG. The Isis had a poor reputation before the war but there was nothing wrong with this one. It was quiet, comfortable, fast enough for a heavy saloon and, like all the pre-war 6-cylinder Morrises, nicely appointed inside.

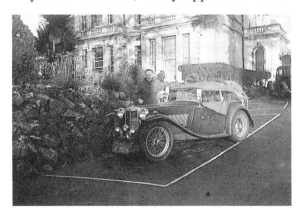

Despite the howls of protest from the traditional MG enthusiast caused by the introduction of the T-Series cars in 1936, there is no doubt that they were much more practical for all-round road and mild competition use than their OHC predecessors. We used this TC in the first post-war long distance rally, the Daily Express 1000 mile run to Torquay and this photograph is taken at our hotel at the finish. Despite losing no marks on the road section I made rather a mess of the special tests. This experience strengthened my admiration for the pushrod MGs which had originally horrified me with their simple mechanics and spindly brake drums. A very practical range which introduced thousands of enthusiasts worldwide to the joys of motoring "Safety Fast".

Within a few months I had sold the Ariel and bought a Wolseley Hornet coupé. The coachwork was in fine condition but the engine was a bit clapped out so I removed it for a complete overhaul.

I was lucky as a small engineering works I had used before the war still had a set of Hornet pistons, so they rebored it for me and I was soon back in business.

Cars were in short supply and I had many offers for this car, but I was not tempted until a friend of mine was sent abroad at short notice leaving him desperate to sell his immaculate Ford 8. I couldn't refuse it at the price he was asking, so the Hornet went to a young man who had been one of the most persistent in trying to buy it.

Business gradually picked up as things slowly moved back to normal. We continued to get cars out of storage, took on more mechanics and a storekeeper. The parts situation was bad but somehow we managed to cope. John Heath had many friends in the neighbourhood who brought their cars in and almost every day one of my old customers would turn up, pleased as punch to see a familiar face. The cars were a mixed bag; the first car I drove when I returned was an Austin 10 but, as we completed overhauling the vehicles removed from storage, I was back driving good quality and highly desirable machinery again.

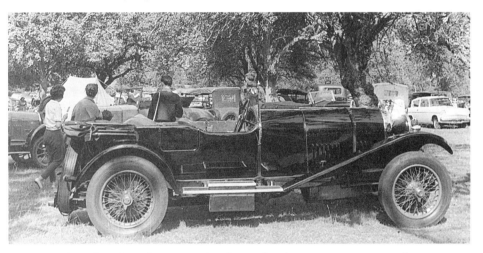

There are those for whom the vintage Bentley is the ultimate sporting car and it is easy to understand why. For myself I prefer the first W O Bentley type – the 3-litre, for its beautiful balance and ease of handling. The 4½ litre and later Speed Six and 8-litre models were of course vastly superior in straight line speed but the little 3-litre in my mind combines all the best qualities of WO's masterpieces.

Very soon the partners were out buying cars for resale, all high class stuff including several Bugattis, a make which had escaped me before the war. One of them was a Type 57S coupé, beautiful in dark metallic grey. It was purchased in the winter from somewhere in the North. On the way back weather conditions were so bad it had to be left at a garage in either Grantham or Stamford, I forget which now. On returning to collect it the engine was frozen solid, resulting in a sheared water pump drive immediately the engine was started. This was soon put right and the car back on the road where it performed impeccably. Eventually it went back North and was sold to a fellow who painted 'Mademoiselle Flo' on each side, which I thought was a bit much.

Another Bugatti was a 57SC Atalante coup in dark blue, another fabulous car on the road. I have models of both these cars in my collection and still admire their beautiful lines. Incidentally, the first one was unblown but the Atalante was supercharged.

We also had a Type 59 3.3 GP Bugatti the ex Charlie Martin Brooklands outer circuit car. Abecassis drove it in several UK events with some success, including winning an invitation race for the six fastest cars at Gransden Lodge and a 2nd FTD at Shelsley Walsh. Fitted with sketchy wings and a silencer it made a terrific road car especially as the roads were nowhere as busy as they are now. This car was also unfortunate enough to get frozen, resulting in a crack down the middle of the head between the two camshafts.

John Heath, who was without a doubt the best mechanic I have ever known, made a beautiful repair, first drilling and pegging the crack then making up a plate from 3/16in steel to cover the whole of the section between the two camshafts. With eight holes machined out to clear the plugs, dozens of countersunk screws all exactly flush and the whole lot chromium plated it was a superb job. We eventually sold the car to Ken Bear and it was

Abecassis had a Type 59 3.3-litre Grand Prix car sold to British racing driver Charlie Martin by Ettore Bugatti in 1936. By any standards the Type 59 has to be the ultimate "vintage" racing car and apart from looking the part it had tremendous performance. For something as transitory as a hill climb George doesn't bother with a crash hat or helmet but tucks in his tie and buttons his jacket against the elements. We had wings and a silencer for the Type 59 which was a treat to drive on the road. This car was sadly the example in which Ken Bear was killed in Jersey in 1946. I had a painting of the car at Prescott driven by Bear which is now in the possession of his widow.

Yet another Bugatti Type 59 3.3 litre Grand Prix car; this is the beautiful example owned by Rodney Clarke and used as the original for the splendid Burago model. Whereas "our" Type 59 was run on the road with the sketchiest of strip wings, Clarke converted his car with beautifully sculpted fenders front and rear, and proper lights even though there was no more cockpit weather protection than that of a genuine Grand Prix car.

a terrible tragedy when he crashed with fatal results during practice for a race in Jersey. The only other Bugatti I've driven was a Type 55 roadster in red and black, a few years later. This car, AUL 23, was sold to Roy Pierpoint who later made a name for himself racing Ford Galaxies in saloon car racing.

In those first two or three years the racing department of HWM had not been formed and we worked it in with the ordinary garage business. I acted as mechanic at the meetings, drove the back up car with all the tools and spares and generally helped all I could.

Our first meeting was at Elstree with an ERA followed by Gransden Lodge, Prescott and Shelsley with the Bugatti previously mentioned and a 1½-litre Alta. We bought an ex-WD Ford V8 truck to use as a transporter and began to get a but more professional. As I have included a separate chapter on my racing activities, I will not dwell on racing matters here unless they happen to fit in with something else happening at the time. We had retained the Morris and MG agencies and one of the first new cars to come through was a TC MG. In those days we could collect our own cars so I picked it up from Abingdon myself. It was a nice day and I really enjoyed the trip. John Heath was a great Citroën fan and during the war he had specialised in the Light Fifteen and also in the Fiat Topolino. We therefore took up a Citroën agency and became quite well known as Citroën specialists. They were exceptional cars on the road and were aptly named by someone 'the poor man's Bugatti'.

Interesting secondhand cars were being sought all the time. Several Delehayes were purchase, a V12 Lagonda, one or two Zagato bodied Alfa Romeos, both 1750 and 2.3, together with one which was either a 2.6 or 2.9. This was a well known car, AMO 999, fabulous to drive and was driven at Prescott by Abecassis where it performed creditably although it was really

For my money the best continental small sports car is the 1750 Alfa Romeo, here seen with rakish Zagato coachwork. This car passed through our hands before I took this photograph and I had plenty of opportunities to sample both six and eight cylinder Alfas during my years with Abecassis and Heath. The partners would buy any decent sporting Alfa that they saw and we did a steady trade in them. The engine was extremely reliable despite the complication and rather like the Bentley range I preferred the smallest model to its illustrious larger brethren. The 1750 Alfa was the most beautifully balanced car. You hardly needed to steer it consciously but just let it run with a light touch on the wheel. My Alfa driving days were high points in my motoring career.

unsuitable for hill climbing.

My own cars continued to be mundane. One that gave tremendous service was a lhd Austin 8. I had obtained the contract to remove a fleet of company owned Austin 8s and 10s from wartime storage and put them in running order for their reps. They were mostly lhd, having beeb originally intended for export in 1939. The outbreak of war had prevented this so they were put on the home market in 1940, a batch of them being purchased by this particular company. They had all done a small mileage but had not been properly laid up, just dumped as the reps were called up for active service.

I got this contract through an old friend who was an executive of the company and responsible for the transport. He wanted one of these cars for himself but in his position could do nothing about it so between us we worked a little fiddle which resulted in us each having a very cheap Austin 8. I had mine recellulosed in silver and with its red upholstery it looked very smart. Later on I bought a Series E Morris 9 from the same source and under more or less the same circumstances. I had this car painted primrose and black, it looked super but was too conspicuous, especially as it also had a distinctive registration number, FOG 112. I got fed up with people telling me where I had been the previous evening! Another little racket we worked was when the Government abolished the basic patrol ration, effactually putting a stop to pleasure motoring. I had no problems running around locally but any long run could have landed me in trouble, so if ever I wanted to go somewhere my pal would write an official letter instructing me to carry out an inspection on the car run by the rep in that area. The poor Swansea man had so many inspections of his Morris 10 he began to get worried so I had to let him into the plot!

I think a word about this friend of mine would not be out of place. He was one of nature's gentlemen; charming, kind hearted and with a great sense of humour, he would get involved in any dodgy scheme as long as no-one got hurt. He was also a delightful raconteur. One story he told that was typical of him was when, as a pilot in World War One, he was appointed

CO of a fighter station in Northern France. There were a number of u/s aircraft about so he got his fitters to dismantle them and build a serviceable machine with the bits. With fictitious identity letters painted on he flew everywhere, including home to England at weekends to see his fiancée. This went on for months; he was never rumbled and it is a measure of his popularity on the station that no-one gave the game away. Then he got a signal from HQ announcing that a team of senior officers were coming the next day to take an inventory. Panic ensued. Apparently if he had been one aircraft short it wouldn't have mattered, but one over was a different thing altogether. He had his chaps working all night dismantling the plane and burying it. Knowing the man I am quite certain the story is true, so if anyone wants a WW1 fighter there is one buried in Northern France. Sadly he died about twenty years ago but not before he had another go in World War Two.

By the end of 1947 the racing department had become too big to run with the normal business. It now had its own mechanics and the ambitious programme for 1948 meant I could no longer go with the cars to the various events, so I remained at home to look after the shop. I still helped when I could and went to race meetings held at weekends but could not go off for several days during the week. From this small beginning emerged the HWM, now something of a legend, and I shall say more about it later on in this book.

The garage side was also expanding, more customers were coming in and more staff were taken on. One of the new customers was a curly-headed young man who appeared one day in an MG TC. His name was Stephen and we immediately struck up a friendship which has endured to this day. We shared many adventures together and for the last sixteen years he has been my business partner. His name will crop up more than once during the rest of this story.

I did a considerable amount of motoring in TC NG's including the first MCC 1000 mile Rally to Torquay. My co-driver was a young man named John Trower. We got on fine together which was perhaps just as well. Our departure point was Harrogate, giving us a longish run before we even started the Rally. The itinerary took us back to London, Dover, northwards again by a circuitous route to Chester, on to North Wales where we had to climb the notorious Bwlch-y-groes in pitch darkness, south again to Bristol, Weston-super-Mare, through Devon to Torquay. We only had one incident. I was asleep when John braked to a sudden stop, nearly shooting me through tie windscreen. "What was that for?" I asked. He apologised and explained he had to do it to avoid running into a brick wall which had loomed up ahead. Since we were in the middle of a Devon moor with not a single brick in sight we changed places rapidly!

We lost no marks on the road section but didn't do too well in the special tests at the finish, but it was all great fun.

Stephen and I did a few trials and small Rallies in his TC, all one day affairs but very enjoyable.

Another TC belonged to a friend of mine who was assisting me at HWM to gain experience prior to starting his own garage. His was quite standard but happened to be a particularly good one so we entered it for Great

Auclum. With a bit of extra tuning it performed very well. We had two runs each and although not placed didn't disgrace ourselves either. I always thought the TC was a better car than a lot of people reckoned. The steering was probably its weak point and, in fact, Betty Haig once described it as an "affliction". I wouldn't have gone that far but it certainly wasn't the most likeable feature of the car.

My own cars had been swapped around a bit and towards the end of 1947 I was able to purchase a new Ford Prefect. This was my first new car and I was very proud of it. Once it was run in I carried out extensive sound proofing and a few mods, and the result was a much smoother and quieter Prefect than average, fully justifying the effort. Apart from normal use I entered it in trials, driving tests and the night navigation rally organised by the Hants and Berks MC. I kept it for about eighteen months, probably because I couldn't afford to change it.

When I did sell it I decided to have a really good car, something special. I looked at various Alvis, Talbots, Lagondas, etc. I could not afford an immaculate example but wanted a sound car I could do up myself. I finally settled for a 1939 Alvis Speed 25 saloon. It had everything I wanted: IFS, servo brakes, twin exhausts and was equal in specification to most post war cars. I had it re-cellulosed in BRG, rechromed, the woodwork re-polished, new headlining and carpets fitted. I overhauled the mechanics myself. The result was a beautiful car, giving me a social status far beyond my humble means.

In the pre-war years I coveted the 2-litre low chassis Lagonda of which this is a fine example snapped post-war in the Prescott paddock. The Lagonda was beautifully made but too heavy to allow its modest 2-litre 4-cylinder engine to endow it with much speed despite having twin, high camshafts and hemispherical combustion chambers. Lagonda later fitted some with superchargers. This was a wonderful car to drive and typical of the best in vintage motoring.

It so happened I met Hilda, my future wife, whilst I had this car and I used to pull her leg by saying she only went out with me because she thought I had plenty of money. I believe the car is still around. I have an Alvis now and belong to the Alvis Owners' Club. My old Speed 25, DLD

850, is listed in their register but I do not know who owns it. During the pre-Alvis period I still made regular trips to Mumbles. The original four was now down to two, one having emigrated and one was married. Camping on the cliff top no longer appealed to us but The Mermaid was now run by a real character named Dick Williams. He was a great enthusiast, owning a 4½ litre Bentley open 4-seater which was a familiar sight and sound around the locality, so The Mermaid was the obvious place to stay.

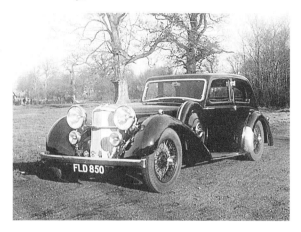

I had a burning ambition to own a really high class car which led me to this Alvis Speed 25. It was wonderful for my ego but its 10mpg fuel consumption was hard on my pocket. It also had an appetite for oil but the high cost of operation was well worth it and faced with the choice I would always prefer to spend money on a good car than on riotous living.

Dick and I became firm friends and we still are, albeit much more subdued. We had some wonderful times there. He was popular in the village and on Saturday nights the bar was crowded with locals, fishermen, sportsmen, villains, shopkeepers and the crew of the Mumbles lifeboat. They would sing as only the Welsh can, we would yarn, swap dirty jokes, gallons of ale would be consumed and after closing time we would all adjourn to his private room for another session. One morning the front page of my daily paper carried news of the loss of the Mumbles lifeboat with all its crew. All those splendid chaps had gone, it just didn't seem possible.

The Alvis eventually departed, sold to an old friend who had been tempting me for a long time, so having had my brief moment of glory I reverted back to an Austin 8, a low mileage post war example in new condition.

Towards the end of 1949 we began to receive the first batch of the new Morris Minors and, not without a bit of a struggle, I persuaded John Heath to let me buy the first convertible. Finished in red with beige hood and trim it looked a picture and was a most delightful little car to drive. Acceleration wasn't its strong point but it would cruise all day at 50–60 which, coupled with the superb roadholding, enabled a good average speed to be maintained on a long run.

It was nicely run in by the following spring so Hilda and I set off on a rather ambitious continental holiday, taking in the French Grand Prix at Reims on the first day. Having survived a terrifying journey to the course during which at least five thousand Frenchmen thought they were Fangio, we watched a wonderful race in brilliant sunshine. Returning to the Minor we were shattered to find the hood has been prised back and Hilda's case stolen. I suppose it was our own fault for leaving it there but all the luggage

When Alec Issigonis' Morris Minor appeared in 1948 it introduced us to new standards in small car roadholding and handling. Unfortunately Issigonis' plans to install a relatively powerful flat four engine were overruled by Lord Nuffield and this, my second new car, an MM Tourer, was fitted with the same gutless sidevalve engine used in my previous Morris Eight. At the time I was running an Austin Eight; the low mileage of which gave it an extremely high value. John Heath having secured one of the much sought-after Minors resisted my attempts to buy it from him on Trade terms; thinking of the £375 retail price that he could easily achieve. Eventually I overcame his resistance by proposing a straight swap for my Austin when Heath's reluctance evaporated in contemplation of the additional £125 profit injection that would result. The Minor did two long continental tours; on one occasion with four up. Here we are in the Swiss Alps which presented no problem provided intelligent use was made of the gearbox in climbing and descending the passes. Eventually, I sold it for twice as much as I paid for it during those years of austerity and the dreaded Covenant.

would not go into the boot. We didn't make the same mistake again. This was not a very good star t, going to the Grand Prix had been my idea and I was not exactly the most popular Englishman in France that day!"

Our spending money was limited by currency regulations but we stopped off in the town to buy the essentials and peace was eventually restored. We went on to Geneva, staying at the hotel I had used previously when over for the Grand Prix des Nations, using it as a base for a few days. A small tour of Switzerland followed, including a trip back over the border to spend a night in Chamonix with some friends who were staying there.

In the course of the run round Switzerland the little Minor climbed the Susten and Furka passes, finally going over the Simplon into Italy. The only trouble experienced was vaporisation of the petrol at high altitudes, not helped by the hot sun and the position of the pump under the bonnet. I resolved it by soaking a cloth in icy water from the little streams running down the rocks and wrapping it round the pump.

Our initial reaction to Italy was not very favourable. It seemed grim and uncared for in direct contrast to Switzerland, but when we ran down into Stresa it was a different world. There were coloured lights along the edge of the lake, it was full of flowers and all very gay (in the meaning of the word in those days).

Having spent the night in a lovely hotel looking over the lake and dined on the most superb roast duck I have ever tasted, we set off in the morning for the south, calling in at Milan and Turin to see the magnificent cathedrals and public buildings. A night in Cuneo then on to the South of France where we stayed in Menton for a few days.

The return journey was made entirely through France, including a night in Avignon where we stood on the famous bridge. The little car behaved impeccably throughout, using no oil and very little petrol. So chuffed were we that next year we did it again, taking two of our friends, but this time we left out Italy. Once more the Morris took it all in its stride, truly a grand little car.

We were still getting plenty of variety in the garage, new cars were coming along but most of the interesting vehicles were late pre-war. One car we saw a bit of was the Railton. I know it was a hybrid with a very "cooking" American engine but it looked good, went extremely well, was fun to drive and I rather enjoyed them.

At one time we had a fire. There was considerable damage and one of the cars burnt out was a nearly new Nash Metropolitan. This car was entirely plastic inside and there is probably nothing with a more pungent, sickly smell than burnt plastic. The car was completely stripped out, cleaned and painted inside, retrimmed with everything new and recellulosed, but the smell remained as strong as ever.

I thought these were dreadful little cars but there were people about who liked them. However, as soon as a prospective purchaser sat inside he didn't want to know. Then one day a fellow came in, a local publican who dabbled in secondhand cars as a sideline and often bought cheap cars from us. He had a real stinking cold and couldn't smell a thing, so in no time at all he had got himself a Metropolitan. Who was it that said there is honour amongst thieves?

In 1950 Stephen bought an MG TD. This was a nice little car, more civilised than the TC but a bit heavier and not quite as much fun. In order to pep it up a bit he had a blower fitted with a fairly low boost, but it made a difference. We did the odd trial in it and I ran it at Great Auclum. We also entered it for a race at Goodwood, of which more anon. At the start of operations after the war John Heath, who had associations with Lagonda, obtained the agency. It was known that a new car was in the pipeline, a luxury saloon of advanced specification and inspired by the great W O Bentley. The last fact alone was sufficient to generate interest and even at this early stage provisional orders were received. Before it went into production David Brown purchased the company, and, having previously bought Aston Martin, co-ordinated manufacture of the two at the Aston Martin works in Feltham. We therefore became distributors for both.

The first post-war Aston, later designated the DB1, was introduced in 1948, a 2-litre, 4-cylinder car with the Claude Hill designed pushrod ohv engine, coil springs all round and a unique chassis consisting of a steel box section tube with side frames to give rigidity. A prototype had won the 24 hour race at Spa so we looked forward to receiving the production cars. When it appeared it sported a handsome drophead coupé body, was well appointed and, in spite of a weight of well over a ton, it had a good performance. The only criticism I can recall was that the body leaked water, an irritating fault on any car. I seem to remember it didn't sell particularly well but it was liked by people who bought them. I know we bought the entire stock (about six cars) when production ceased.

The Lagonda came out a bit later, around 1948–9. The *Motor* tested a DHC in 1949, recording a top speed of 90 mph, pretty good going in those days for a luxury motor car.

The specification truly was advanced, twin ohc, wet liners, IRS as well as IFS and several other features not found in British cars at that time. I suppose it would be true to say it was not a successful motor car, giving a considerable amount of trouble. One of the most consistent engine faults was blown head gaskets, caused by the liners sinking below the level of the block face. On the early engine, designated the 'L' series and later on the 'V' series the liners were sealed by thin figure-of-eight gaskets at the bottom. They varied in thickness and were selected for each pair of liners to bring each one 0.04" above the face of the block. An improvement was made later by making the gaskets of copper and later still, on the 'D' series engines, the liners had a flange at the top and were sealed with an O-ring.

In fairness this trouble was not confined to the Lagonda engine, it being fairly common on most wet liner designs. There were other irritating faults in the car, many of them not serious but niggling to a person who had just paid out a lot of money. Their biggest problem was the same one that affected every maker of this sort of car, they just couldn't compete with Jaguar.

I know I will not be popular with a lot of people, but I have to say the Mk VII Jaguar was a better car. The purists will point to the Lagonda's advanced specification, its hand built construction, its racing pedigree, but the fact remains that if you wanted a fast, quiet, luxurious and, above all, reliable car you had to buy a Mk VII. What is more you could keep your wife's hands off it by buying a small car for her with the money you saved!

Of all Astons I much prefer the Sixes to the V8 and of the Sixes my favourite is without question the very first model; the DB2. Here my friend Stephen's DB2 is snapped in the Cotswold village of Ducklington, one of the prettiest in Oxfordshire. Hilda and I took every opportunity to enjoy Aston motoring and I count myself more than fortunate to have had the regular use of such cars which I never grew tired of driving. In its day the DB2 could handle better than anything else I can think of. The suspension and steering were absolutely right and only an idiot could get into trouble with one. The gearbox was delightful, the engine wonderfully smooth and powerful and the DB2 takes my vote for the most fabulous car I know. Sadly as with many models, the Aston grew up and lost much in the process.

The Aston was a different proposition. In 1949 the DB2 was born with a sports saloon body. Three cars were built for Le Mans and one of them had the Lagonda engine. It retired early on but the seeds were sown for the advent of one of Britain's greatest cars. I first drove one in 1950. Astons had started torace seriously and George Abecassis was one of the team drivers. One Sunday morning he brought his team car round to the garage and told me I could "whip it round the block". I didn't need to be told twice! Stephen was with me so we both jumped in and set off on a good blind. We were so thrilled with it that the "block" extended for about ten miles and we brought it back with reluctance.

On learning that more civilised versions were to be put into production Stephen ordered one and just before Easter in 1952 I collected it from the works in Feltham. Finished in dark green it looked a picture, obviously not as potent as the team car but fast enough and with the same fabulous handling qualities.

I had some wonderful runs with this car, both as a passenger with Stephen, a first class driver, and when I borrowed the car myself. There were few about at that time and it was impossible to stop without a crowd gathering. In August Hilda and I tool it to Lynmouth, staying at the Bath Hotel for the weekend. On the following Saturday the flood disaster struck Lynmouth.

My love of Aston Martins is not confined to the post-war models and here is a delightful long chassis 1½-litre spotted at Prescott. I much preferred the short chassis versions of the car even though these were still far too heavy for the modest power output available. The Ulster, short chassis Mk.2 and International were delightful cars to drive with a seemingly unburstable engine which kept the car moving effortlessly once speed had built up. The gearbox had to be mastered but like every other element of the car was beautifully engineered and a joy to operate.

Amongst the other devastation, all the cars in the Bath car park were washed out to sea. One week earlier and Stephen's beloved Aston would have been with them.

I had the use of two other DB2s during 1952–3, one car, a Vantage, SPL 450, is still about. Green with beige trim when I saw it last, it was originally black with red. I ran it in for the owner and subsequently used it quite a lot. The third one was a drop head. It had suffered the usual head gasket trouble but it had not been spotted before water got into the sump resulting in the need to strip the engine. After the rebuild I had another running-in session and shortly afterwards the owner was sent abroad for an indefinite period by his company. Not wishing to lay it up he asked me to keep it for him and use it regularly. This was too good to be true! My own personal Aston – and I was not a bit upset when his stay abroad lasted a long time.

Meanwhile, down at Mumbles, my pal Dick Williams (known locally as Dick the Fish) had forsaken his vintage Bentleys after having owned four, all open $4\frac{1}{2}$-litres. At a recent race meeting at Lulsgate at which I also competed, he had put a rod through the side which may have had something to do with it.

Probably because of my lyrical praise of the DB2, he bought one. I went down to see it – as good a reason as any – and found it to be in excellent condition. It was fitted with the original cast iron brake drums but for some time I had been jealously guarding a set of Alfins. These improved the brakes considerably although sometimes it was a job to stop them squealing. I promised them to him which, of course, meant another trip down there to fit them. Dick has never been without an Aston since and still has one today.

During 1950 George Abecassis attended a function in London and found himself next to Lt. Gen. Sir Frederick Browning, Comptroller of HRH Princess Elizabeth's household. The conversation naturally turned to cars and the General was complaining he could never get his car properly serviced. George promptly stepped in, suggesting we looked after him. His car was a pre-war 2-litre MG DHC and he thought the world of it. He had an intense dislike of chrome and the whole car was painted dark blue, radiator, bumpers, lamps, even the knock on hub caps, surely one of the first examples of what the manufacturers now call "Colour Coding". He was so pleased with our service he told Cmdr. Michael Parker, the Duke's equerry, and very soon we were doing his car as well.

This eventually led to us looking after the personal cars – as distinct from the State cars – of Their Royal Highnesses Prince Philip and Princess Elizabeth. I went up to Clarence House and met the head chauffeur. I had been there previously but only to the administrative offices, but this time went to the house. As a measure of the difference between then and now Prince Charles, then about two, was in his pram in the garden and I was allowed to go up and talk to him. I doubt if one could get within a mile of a Royal baby now.

I returned with the Austin Sheerline that had been one of their wedding presents, but before doing so had to drive the chauffeur round the block. I obviously passed his test as he got out and let me go solo.

We continued to service their cars for several years. One car I remember

My idea of a successful big car is that it should feel smaller when you sit in it. This was certainly not the case for the Austin Sheerline or its coachbuilt sister the VDP Princess which was even more cumbersome than the basic model from which it derived. I didn't dislike them however and they were honest, modestly priced limousines. This is a rather special specimen belonging to HRH Princess Elizabeth and the Duke of Edinburgh and I was privileged to be responsible for its maintenance together with that of several other cars in the Royal Household. The connection came from a chance conversation between George Abecassis and General Browning, Comptroller of the Royal Household at a dinner and at the time we were not allowed to make mention of our prestigious responsibility. Nevertheless the news got around . . .

with affection was a Mk 1 Ford Zephyr which Prince Philip used. It looked perfectly standard, but went like a rocket.

When the King died and they moved into Buckingham Palace I had to go to the Royal Mews. This is a fascinating place containing many old Royal cars, mostly Daimlers, the Queen Mother's old Lanchesters, the horse-drawn carriages used for State occasions, the Coronation coach and many other interesting items covering Royal transport over many generations. As we all know, the State cars are painted in a deep sort of maroon but the personal cars were in a beautiful shade of bottle green, including the straight eight Rolls Royce which they had at that time. It is the only one I have ever seen. I wasn't allowed to drive it but was once taken to Waterloo Station in it. I felt very important!

The Duke was President of the AA and all his cars had a special badge. There was at that time an AA box at the top of Paines Hill in Cobham. It was always manned and I would purposely drive past it to get one of the best salutes to be seen outside the Brigade of Guards.

I once collected the Sheerline on a Saturday morning. Forgetting there was an International at Twickenham I came home along the Great Chertsey Road and was soon snarled up in a long line of stationary cars. In the glove compartment was a card addressed to the Police stating that the car was on Royal business and that every assistance should be given to its occupants. With visions of my lunch getting cold I fished it out and showed it to a motorcycle policeman. In a flash I was being escorted past the stationary traffic feeling very smug.

One day I was in my office when the 'phone rang. It was Michael Parker speaking from the Royal Mint. Apparently Prince Philip was making a tour of the place prior to joining the Queen at Badminton. As he went in he said to Parker: "ring up that fellow Hobbs, tell him I want an Aston Martin drophead up here for when I come out". "How long will that be?" I asked and was told "about an hour". This was a stinker. I knew he was contemplating a new car and could have been thinking of an Aston but we didn't have one.

I rang the factory at Feltham, but the only one there was David Brown's personal car. They dare not lend that out, even to the Duke of Edinburgh, without his permission and he was in the South of France. Heath and Abecassis were away so I couldn't enlist their support so I pleaded with them to contact him. About fifteen minutes later they rang to say I could have it. Whilst I went home to change, our driver went to Feltham to collect it. I rang Michael Parker at the Mint, saying I would be there as soon as possible. He told me to take it straight to the Palace, to ignore speed limits as I only had half an hour and, if stopped, to tell the police I had an urgent appointment at Buckingham Palace with the Duke of Edinburgh. I could imagine the average copper's reaction to that one but went flat out anyway. I arrived just in time, the sentries had been warned and waved me straight in. As I went in a side door the Duke came in through the front. I hadn't met him before and he was most charming, shook hands and thanked me for all I had done. We went outside and I showed him round the car. He was wearing a dark blue suit and as he got in he put on a chauffeur's cap, his detective sat beside him wearing a bowler and they roared off to Badminton looking like business man and chauffeur.

After about a week the Palace rang for me to pick up the car "and would I lay on a Lagonda drophead?" The Lagonda by then was a much better car and the engine was now a 3-litre. David Brown had bought Tickfords who had produced a much nicer body. There was no panic for this one, I was to take it to Windsor Castle in two day's time. I had to borrow Mrs David Brown's car for this session. She was happy to let me have it and at the appointed time I presented myself at Windsor Castle. I left it with Cmdr. Parker and Group Captain Peter Townsend as the Duke hadn't arrived, but first gave them a run round Windsor Great Park. It is fairly well known that the Duke bought one. There was no publicity in fact, and although all the paper work went through us we didn't hand it over. By the peculiar rules of the motor trade all our Aston and Lagonda sales had to go through the factory main distributors, in this case Brooklands of Bond Street. They seized on this one and in spite of all my hard work I didn't get a look in.

Soon after this we gave up the Royal work. The Lagonda was naturally serviced by the factory, the other cars were gradually being absorbed into the normal Buckingham Palace maintenance set up so we reckoned it was time to bale out. It was an extremely interesting and pleasant interlude in the ordinary routine and, being intensely pro Royal Family and all that it stands for, I view those few years with a certain amount of pride.

Amongst my treasured possessions are a coloured photo of the Queen on horseback in a folder which was given to me and an official Buckingham Palace Christmas card.

While all this was going on the DB2 had grown into the DB2/4, basically the same car but a bit longer to accommodate two small rear seats, stronger

If I had never driven the DB2 I would have appreciated the DB2/4 Mk.3 more easily.
However, it had lost some of the balance of the DB2 although its lines were still elegant
and a drophead alternative was now available.

bumpers and a few other minor alterations. It was a good move, giving the car a wider market and, as it *could* be called a four seater, it was easier to justify it as a company car.

It still drove and handled better than anything else but somehow the magic had gone out of it when compared with the DB2. We sold a good number of these and more still later on when it was fitted with the 3-litre engine, but it wasn't all smiles and bouquets.

One elderly company chairman had a front suspension housing break when on a business trip to Germany. He could have had a nasty accident and was a bit upset. Another one was sold to an engineer in Uxbridge, rather an aggressive sort of character but a good chap underneath. His car was painted ice blue and really looked a picture. The first weekend after taking delivery he went for a long run, calling at a garage on the way back for petrol. The Aston was much admired by several people at the garage and one of them asked to see the engine. As most of you probably know, the bonnet on these cars consisted of the complete front assembly, wings, lamps, etc., and was hinged at the front. As he opened it there was a sharp crack and the whole lot fell into the road. Both hinges had snapped. The admiration of the bystanders turned to mickey taking and he was furious.

The car went back to the factory and was delivered back to him the following weekend. He had got over his annoyance and could even see the funny side of it. He became a very good customer, buying some cars for his company and a new Rover 100 for himself. One day he asked me if I could spare some Sunday mornings to take his wife out in the Aston and teach her high speed driving. I was delighted to oblige as she was a lovely girl and how often does a man with a pretty wife ask you to take her out? She was a very sensible person, already a good driver and proved a good pupil, so after about six sessions I reluctantly told him there was no more I could teach her, all she now needed was experience.

After the initial drama this car turned out to be a very good one. One day he telephoned me from hngis weekend cottage in Norfolk asking if I would mind collecting the Aston from his house and taking it up to him. I left very early on the Sunday morning to avoid the traffic and had a marvellous run.

In fairness to Astons the failures previously described were isolated incidents; generally speaking the cars were very well put together. It was handy being so near the factory. I spent a lot of time there, got to know everyone and was given complete run of the works. I got to know all the snags, any mods. that were pending and many things that were not only interesting but useful to me in setting up what I believed was the best Aston Service Dept. outside the factory. They were a jolly decent crowd and made me feel like one of the family.

The DB 2/4 was replaced by the Mk 3, very similar in appearance except for the front and instrument panel. It also had disc front brakes and it took a little time to sort out the correct front/rear braking ratio. At first it was easy to lock the front wheels resulting in the press-on types going straight over roundabouts.

We sold a drophead to a London businessman who asked me to run it in. Hilda was spending a few days at her home in Penrith. I had arranged to collect her at the weekend and managed to organise it so that the Aston was just about run in for the trip. I set off early Saturday morning, the previous afternoon had seen the opening of Britain's first motorway, the Preston by-pass section of the M6.

Instead of the usual A1 Scotch Corner route to Penrith I went up the West side, joining the motorway at its commencement. Sitting at the entrance were two policemen in a patrol car. Seeing the Aston and seeing me grinning, they no doubt guessed what I had in mind and grinned back (a bit different today!). I had a flat out blind all the way; after the normal roads it was really something and all legal too.

I found the Mk 3, like its predecessors, a wonderful car to drive. Just before coming to this part of my story the current issue of 'Classic and Sportscar' carried one of their excellent 'Back to Back' articles wherein they compare two cars of similar type, in this case the Mk 3 Aston and Jaguar XK150. To my surprise there were adverse comments on the Aston's handling. I am a great Jaguar fan, I own three at the moment and hope to devote a separate chapter to them later on in this book. Although not one of my favourite Jaguars, there is no doubt that the XK150 is a fantastic car, but having driven a lot of each at the time they were more or less current models I wouldn't hesitate to say the Aston was the nicest car to drive. Honour is satisfied, however, as they go on to quote Roy Salvadori who is full of praise for the Aston. There is no doubt Roy was one of the outstanding sports car drivers of the day, and also he wouldn't write what he didn't think was true, so his comments are valuable.

One Saturday morning I received a call from Dick Williams. He had shunted his DB2, could I come down and look at it? Apart from clean cars in the showroom there was only one car in the place suitable for a fast 200 mile run and that was a 3-litre 2/4 drophead belonging to David Brown's daughter, Angela. Permission to borrow it was sought and granted. I went home, picked up Hilda and the dog, shoved a few things in an overnight bag and had the best run to Mumbles I've had before or since.

I make no apologies for including another picture of my favourite Aston – in this case Robin Grant's DB2 fitted with Vantage engine and three Weber carbs. I ran in the car for him and even at modest bedding in speeds the performance was all that one could desire.

There were still no motorways, so it was all normal road driving with towns and villages and Saturday afternoon traffic but we did it in just over four hours. I did an estimate for the repairs on the Sunday morning and we left for home after lunch. In due course the Aston was sent up on a trailer and repaired.

Another really outstanding Aston was the DB3S. George Abecassis was still in the works team and often brought one home. I never missed the chance to drive one – they were terrific. Later on a few were sold to the public and we had one or two. We converted one to a proper road car with a windscreen, interior trim, quieter exhaust and other refinements for Tony Oldsworth, a Lloyd's Underwriter, International rally driver and keen member of the Aston Martin Owners' Club. I remember him clearly because he pinched my DB3S workshop manual and my special plug spanner. If you happen to read this, Tony, all is forgiven!

A little car that gave me a lot of fun was the Isetta. We took up the agency soon after the BMW-built version was imported into the UK. For some time I ran the demonstrator, it was a jolly handy little vehicle for local running around; apart from the economy it could be parked wherever there were a few feet of space, often nose on to the kerb. It was remarkably strong. We had a salesman at the time who was a bit too fond of the booze and one night he rolled it. Waking up in hospital with an outside headache but otherwise undamaged, he discharged himself, rapidly searched around, found the car and drove home. Neither he or the Isetta were much the worse for the incident.

4
FROM THE FIFTIES TO 1966

I seem to have devoted a lot of space to Aston Martin towards the end of the last chapter, partly because they were wonderful cars and partly because I was so involved with them. This involvement continued until the early Sixties when, although we still handled Astons, my own time was more or less fully taken up with the Facel Vega.

There were other cars in my life and my own changed frequently, but for much of the time I was able to use other cars to the extent that I didn't need one of my own. One car I remember was a lhd Packard V12, the only one I have seen. It was well pre-war, I would think about 1937-8, a four door convertible. In American terminology I believe it would be called a Phaeton. To drive it was a revelation, nothing I had previously driven was anything like it. Another 12-cylinder car I drove was a Phantom III Rolls Royce with an owner driver close coupled saloon body. It belonged to the owner of the

Singers have never enjoyed the same reputation as the rival MG and Riley sports cars. However, Singer made several attempts to upgrade their image and this 6 cylinder 1½ litre Works car was produced to very high standards although only half a dozen or so were made. The crankshaft and con rods were designed and made to "ERA standard" and the car had excellent performance. I should have kept this very underrated motor car and enjoyed some pleasure from all my hard work in rebuilding it.

DB2 SPL 450 and was a beautiful car, heavier to drive than the Packard but with that indefinable quality that makes Rolls Royce so special.

Some time previously I had stripped out and rebuilt an MG K3 as I have described in the racing chapter, but that had been sold and I had nothing to play with, as it were. One day I was told about a 1½-litre 6-cylinder Singer Le Mans for sale in Whitstable. I had always fancied one of these, so although it was pretty rough I bought it. I dismantled it for a complete rebuild, overhauling the chassis as the first step. The body was made good and painted prior to refitting. In those days people were not concerned with originality, so the first thing I did was to scrap the beautiful but very heavy wings and running boards, making up some lightweight close fitting wings and stays. The engine was basically sound, the crankshaft was a lovely piece of work in perfect condition and there was very little bore wear.

I was doing all the work in the evenings after the garage was closed but some of the racing chaps were there and Alf Francis took a great interest, offering to modify the head for better performance. He designed and had made a set of tulip inlet valves and worked out how much could be planed off the head to raise the compression. He suggested a solid copper head gasket and had that made for me too. I fitted new rings, and although the pistons were worn where the gudgeon pin goes through, we decided to leave it as the pistons would expand and a bit of extra clearance might not be a bad thing.

Eventually the big day came when I pressed the starter. There was a clatter as all my lovely new inlet valves hit the pistons. A check of the valve timing revealed that to be correct, so the only conclusion was that too much had been planed off the head. Having removed it again I found that, in spite of careful annealing and tightening down, the copper gasket had leaked all the water into the sump. Although he had a somewhat abrasive manner, Alf was a sensitive chap and was most upset, offering to pay for the valves. I wouldn't hear of it; we all slip up sometimes. It was good of him to help in the first place and I had to take some of the blame, anyway.

I didn't say anything as there was always a certain amount of friction between the racing dept. and the workshop and I had no wish to stir anything up. I completely lost interest in the project and as my back was playing me up at the time, one of the fitters finished it off and I sold it. In those days the phrase "You can't win 'em all" wasn't around, but it applied just the same.

Interesting cars were still coming along. I had very little to do with Ferraris but we did have one for a period, an open two seater. I believe it was called a Barchetta but my knowledge of Ferrari types is about on a par with my knowledge of Bugatti. I do remember this one had a racing history, having been driven in many international events, including Le Mans, by the late Tom Cole. Be that as it may, it was a fabulous car on the road with terrific performance but quite docile with it. Over the years I have driven several others, including a 2+2, a Daytona and a GTO and they have a fascination all of their own. I have attended three meetings of the Ferrari Owners' Club as a spectator and the sight of around 150 Ferraris, most of them red, is unforgettable.

It was my pleasure to enjoy driving several different Ferraris of the golden period of the V12. This is the 225 Sport with Vignale body driven by Tom Cole at Le Mans in 1952. With a 2.7 litre V12 the performance was impressive to say the least although the fact that Ferrari used a conventional rear axle with so much power it a tricky car to handle;

even on the roads around Walton-on-Thames. My Alsatian Jimpy is waiting to accompany me and Hilda on a run and although there cannot be many dogs taken for a Sunday afternoon walk in a Le Mans Ferrari, Jimpy was not impressed.*

I did a lot of motoring in Jaguars but, as mentioned previously, I shall cover that later on. At the same time we took up an agency for one of their competitors, Armstrong Siddeley. We were more or less in at the start of the Sapphire, a large luxurious car with a rather unique 3.4-litre 6 cylinder engine. It had a high mounted camshaft and inclined push rod ohv. It was a good solid car, originally available with a choice of manual or pre-selector gearboxes, but later on a full automatic was added to the range. I did a lot of miles in them, found them a little cumbersome for ordinary motoring but excellent on a long run.

I remember one particularly pleasant trip. We had purchased Mrs David Brown's Lagonda DHC and re-sold it to a shipbuilding character on the Clyde. I arranged to deliver it to his office at Port Glasgow, and took Hilda and the dog, spending the night in Penrith and leaving them there whilst I went on the following day. The part exchange car was a Sapphire, one of the rare four light saloons and the run home was very enjoyable. Later on Armstrongs brought out smaller versions, the 6-cylinder 236 and the 4-cylinder 234. These were not a great success and the new 2.4 Jaguar killed them stone dead.

A few Austin Healeys and Triumph TR2s came my way, both nice cars to drive but I couldn't get excited about them. The MGA was real fun. I sold a secondhand Aston to another friend in Mumbles, taking his MGA fixed head coupé in part exchange. He was a fanatic and his cars were always perfect. I met him somewhere near Gloucester to make the swap and the run back in the MG so impressed me I used it until it was sold. Another unusual car I drove a lot was a Marauder owned by a relation of Stephen. This was a very pleasant open two seater of a sporting nature rather than an out-and-out sports car. Based almost entirely on Rover 75 parts it provided good performance motoring with comfort and a remarkable lack of noise.

I have always had a soft spot for the Talbots of Georges Roesch. This is one of the Fox and Nichol team Talbot 105s now in the care of Anthony Blight. At the time that I took this snap it was owned by Charles Mortimer but I had driven it earlier and marvelled at the performance of its modest looking pushrod ohv 6-cylinder 3-litre engine which embodied all the sacred principles expounded so regularly and clearly in the correspondence columns of the motoring press by its designer. The chassis appeared to be very straightforward but provided the car with amazingly good roadholding and braking.

The makers had removed the free wheel, which was a standard fitment on the Rover at that time, and cunningly inserted an overdrive in its place. The result was really effortless cruising.

The post-war Rileys were very good cars. The $1\frac{1}{2}$-litre RME and the $2\frac{1}{2}$-litre RMF were handsome vehicles with lusty 4-cylinder engines, rack and pinion steering and excellent handling. I can never understand why these cars are so undervalued today by collectors, especially when people go mad over sit-up-and-beg Populars and the like. Performance of the $2\frac{1}{2}$-litre was exceptional for a fairly heavy car and, providing careful attention was paid to tyre pressures, they were very sure-footed. Two of them were campaigned regularly in sports and saloon car races and were very seldom unplaced.

We had a nice RME for sale and one morning a man arrived in a chauffeur-driven Daimler. He had seen it advertised and felt it was just what he wanted. He was a bit rough and ready but well dressed in casual clothes and looked what he said he was, a sheep farmer.

He wanted to pay by cheque and take the car away which was at the best of times a dodgy business, so he gave us the telephone number of his bank and the name of the manager. This character said there was no problem, he was rolling in money and dead honest. So what with this, his chauffeur driven car and his general air of affluence, he was allowed to take it. Of

*To remind me of my connection with war time aircraft and my love of all fine mechanical
things I must include a shot of my favourite aircraft, the Spitfire; this example on
exhibition at Beaulieu. For so many of us who were grown men during the 1939-45 war
the Spitfire symbolises the RAF and the spirit of the Battle of Britain without which the
adventures described in my book (and many other things) would have never taken place.
If I need justification for including this photograph I will quote the Rolls-Royce engine
behind the prop.*

course it was a stolen cheque, the Daimler was hired, the "bank manager"
was an accomplice and his address was fictitious, so we had been conned.
It turned out he was known to the police and had a record. He was eventually
caught and after several months we got our Riley back. However, there was
more drama to come. Through one of our local customers the car was sold
to a titled lady in the Scottish Highlands. It was one of those feudal set
ups. She owned the entire district, farms, villages, the lot; everybody had
to obey her commands and they were all scared stiff of her. One day an
observant policeman recognised the number as being on his stolen car list
and stopped the car. He nearly had a fit when he saw who was driving,
but had to go through with it and told her she was driving a stolen car.
She took him apart well and truly and there was a frightful fuss over it.
She wasn't too pleased with us either for selling her a car that had been
stolen and we were glad she lived about 400 miles away.

    We had another car stolen, an XK 140. To open the showroom doors
was neither an easy or quiet task as they were old and tended to jam in
their channels, but someone did it in the night, moved several cars out of
the way and took this Jaguar from the back. They then put the other cars
back on their spots and closed the doors. All without being disturbed.
Nothing was heard of it for several months and then we had a call from
the police in Gainsborough to say they had it in their yard.

The Brighton run was something I never missed and these shots taken from the same vantage point show a couple of delightful veterans including some of later vintage acting as tenders.

It had been found abandoned with a burned-out coil and another car stolen from the same place. It was on false number plates and it had taken the police a while to trace the car back to us. I went up there with a new coil and a pair of plates with the correct number on to bring it back. I was amazed when I saw it. I expected it to be scruffy and bashed about; not only was it immaculate inside and out but there was a service book in the glove box which showed it had recently had a major service. They never caught the thief as far as I know and I can't help feeling he deserved to get away with it for his cheek.

About this time a fellow in his mid-twenties started coming in regularly with a seemingly never-ending supply of Hillman Minx and Humber Hawks. I got friendly with him and it transpired he was employed by the Rootes Group on the wholesale sales side. One day when he came in he said he had a fleet of cars to run in prior to them being sent out as demonstrators, but it would take two or three months and would I help him out. He suggested I take a car, use it for 5-600 miles and then swap it for another one, all petrol to be charged to him.

I couldn't go wrong on this one. Although the cars were not the most exciting things on four wheels they were new, comfortable and the Hawk had a marvellous heater, a good point in December. It was just about the time Rootes had abandoned their old side valve engine, brought out a new ohv unit and a sleek body shape. I got to like the Hawk and still think it was a nicer looking car than the bulbous style that succeeded it. If you accepted the fact that it was a roomy family saloon and didn't try to chuck it about like an MG it was quite good on the road.

Amongst other interesting cars I drove in this period were Daimler Conquest and Century, Alvis 3-litre, Jensen 541, Jowett Jupiter and the MG TF. The latter was to be the last of the illustrious T-series, although we didn't know it at the time. A little saloon I also liked was the MG YB. We dabbled in Healeys for a bit and I loved the Silverstone, a beefy sports car with little in the way of personal comforts but which stuck to the road like glue. At that time we were doing a considerable amount of work for Charles Mortimer. He had an exciting collection of cars and at one stage bought a $4\frac{1}{2}$-litre low chassis Invicta. We had it in to cure an oil leak from between the block and the crankcase. When it was finished I tested it. I hadn't driven an Invicta since well before the war; it was one of my favourites then and it was pure magic to drive one again.

Our original Sales Manager had departed and his place was taken by a man who liked unusual cars, preferably continental. We had just the thing for him, a 1939 1100 cc Hotchkiss, originally designed and built as an Amilcar but gaining a Hotchkiss badge when that company took over the Amilcar concern.

It was a pretty little four seater convertible, very advanced mechanically with front wheel drive, independent suspension and other features that put it ahead of its time. The engine was badly worn and parts were impossible

I have included this snap of an early tram to remind me that I hit one with a flat-nosed Morris Oxford in 1931. Under the circumstances I think that a good tram is a tram in captivity.

to obtain so John Heath fitted a Ford 10 unit. Fitting an engine from a rear wheel drive car to one with fwd was not an easy task and involved a lot of work. John did everything himself, made up engine bearers, an adaptor plate for the bellhousing, sundry pipes, water ducts, etc., and the whole thing was beautifully done, absolutely professional.

The car was re-cellulosed in pale silver grey with a grey hood and the sales manager took it over. He became very fond of that little car and it served as his personal transport until the day he ran off with the wife of one of our customers, but that is another story!

We continued to sell and service Citroëns. John Heath got hold of a lhd 6-cylinder with the registration number JBH 8. It had considerable body damage on one side but JBH were his initials so it was repaired for him to use. Whether it was coincidence or because it was a French-built one I do not know, but we all agreed it was the best Citroën Six to drive we had come across.. He sold it eventually to an RAF type connected with the Royal Household, but kept the number.

Another car I enjoyed driving was a Lagonda LG 6 DHC. I think it was a 1938 model. These Lagondas were solid, luxurious cars but had a good performance and felt a true thoroughbred. The coachwork was similar to

With all due respect to W O Bentley and despite its excellent qualities, I always preferred the 16/80 or M45 Lagondas to this LG6. The LG6 had a feeling of real quality about it that was very satisfying and gave an impression of great strength. The performance was good and although I enjoyed driving it, to my "vintage" mind it was "lacking" in some difficult-to-define way.

some fitted with the V12 and I believe the chassis was much the same too. I only drove two of the pre-war V12s, both saloons, and must confess I saw very little advantage in them over the 6. Obviously they were more powerful and more refined, but whether the difference was enough to justify the additional first cost and running expenses was, I suppose, a question of personal choice. I remember hearing at the time that they were prone to catch fire. The carburettor was in the middle of the vee over the ignition system and, if it flooded or leaked, up she went. I never drove a Rapide much to my regret.

Things progressed in normal fashion; good cars came and went, bad cars came and went, until the fateful day when John Heath succumbed to injuries received in the 1956 Mille Miglia.

It was a dreadful blow to us all; he was undoubtedly the guiding light in the organisation and although he could be difficult at times it didn't last. John was a mixture of generosity and meanness. I have known him go mad over a washer left lying on the floor, I have seem him go to great lengths to remove an unfranked stamp from an envelope and I have known him, without hesitation, give one of the chaps £25 – a lot of money in those days – because he was in trouble. It took a little time for things to settle down but eventually it did. George Abecassis invited me to join him on the Board as Service Director and we gradually got back to normal. The racing side was slowly run down, the cars were sold, but a partly completed chassis made into a road going sports coupé.

We were still very much involved with Aston Martin and one exciting, but unfortunately not very successful design, to come out of Feltham was a new V12 Lagonda. Not unlike a larger DB3S to look at and with a similar chassis layout it was built under the direction of Professor Eberan von Eberhorst. With a capacity of just under $4\frac{1}{2}$-litres it was an impressive machine but there was a fundamental weakness in the design. The barrel-type crankcase was of cast aluminium and the main bearing housings were also

H W Motors acquired the majority of the ex-Works Aston Martin sports racing cars of which this V12 Lagonda is an exciting example. I took this photograph when out on test and I must say that I enjoyed it although there were fundamental errors in design which prevented the car from showing its true promise. Worst feature of all was inadequate bottom end rigidity resulting from the use of aluminium bearing housings within an aluminium crankcase; an arrangement which generated unacceptable clearances in use and a slack bottom end.

aluminium, consequently they had the same rate of expansion when hot, resulting in too much clearance. Had a cast iron crankcase been used as per the Aston L and subsequent engines, the bearing housings would have tightened into it. I believe three cars were built but I only ever saw two. The first car ran at Silverstone finishing 5th; it was then crashed at Le Mans early in the race and later at Silverstone again it was 4th. The following year at Le Mans it retired with fuel trouble. I think it was not long after this that the project was abandoned by Aston. We bought the two complete cars and all the spares.

When they first arrived at the garage I jumped into one and belted up the road, heading for a small stretch nearby that was de-restricted. On the way back I was stopped by a policeman who, attracted by the noise I had made on the way out, was waiting for me. He pointed out that I had no excise licence, no number plates and in various other ways I was breaking the law. I humbly made my excuses, expecting the little black book to come out. Instead he said: "Isn't it a beauty, can I see the engine?" We spent about ten minutes going over the car; he was obviously an enthusiast and was tickled pink at having a close look at a very rare car. He then said: "Here, you had better push off, if another copper comes along he will probably pinch you". So I came smartly back, thankful that some policemen are also car enthusiasts and I had been lucky enough to find one. They really were superb cars to drive, fast, flexible with faultless steering and brakes and impeccable road holding. We sold one to a fellow living in the Bournemouth area who liked these sort of cars and could afford to indulge in them. I never saw it again and have no idea what happened to it after that.

The other one was bought by Noel Cunningham-Reid and we undertook

If the V12 Lagonda could be criticised with justification, the DB3S Aston was hard to fault. A job which required regular testing of such magnificent thoroughbreds kept me happy and I could have driven these wonderful cars all day without complaint. The road behaviour of this DB3S could only be described as impeccable. I can't say anything bad about this car.

to convert it to a more practical road car, similar to the DB3S we had done for Tony Oldsworth. Just about this time a well known racing driver, who had better be nameless, became involved with a coachbuilding company in South London and was continually asking us for work, so we gave him this car to do. It had only been there a few days when I opened the morning paper to read the company was going into liquidation. I rang Abecassis and we agreed I should go up at once to get the car out if it hadn't already been impounded.

I arrived just before they opened; fortunately the chap with the key appeared to know nothing about the plight of his employers and let me take it. I parked it round the corner, rang the garage for someone to bring up trade plates and a driver for my car and got it back home. The spare parts, which included a complete engine, several crankshafts and unmachined castings were advertised. We had one or two enquiries but in particular Norman Buckley, the power boat ace, was interested in putting the engine into one of his boats . He came down but I cannot remember if he bought the engine or not. I never heard of it being fitted to any of his craft so perhaps he didn't.

There were still many pre-war cars about but they had no collectors' value then and were just secondhand cars. One that came into the garage was a 1937 Austin 7 Ruby. It had only done 43,000 miles and I had known it

Hilda and I have owned a succession of dogs including three Alsatians. This is Donna guarding Hilda's first car, a 1937 Austin Seven Ruby renovated by me and given to her as a Christmas present. The Ruby was mechanically very similar to the earlier Austin Seven but fitted with heavy steel coachwork that gave the poor little engine an even harder job of work to do. Nevertheless, provided that 45 mph was an acceptable top speed the Ruby gave economical and reliable transport.

Hilda's second car was this 1936 Wolseley Wasp. The engine was a 4-cylinder version of the Hornet with chain driven single overhead camshaft. Despite its large body it went very well indeed and handled impressively on its large section tyres. The Wasp was a grand little car that we should have kept.

Hilda's next car was a major step forward in time. This Austin A30 gave marvellous service not only to Hilda but also to a friend to whom we sold it later and eventually my nephew who bought it in turn from him. The number plate is probably worth more now than I got for the car when I sold it.

from new, so I bought it as a Christmas present for Hilda. I had it re-cellulosed, re-chromed where necessary and it looked a picture. I said nothing about it and kept it at the garage until Christmas morning when I picked it up on my way home from church. She was taken completely by surprise and couldn't believe it was hers. It was her first car, although she had been able to drive for some years, and it gave her a lot of pleasure.

At that time I knew an old boy with an immaculate Wolseley Wasp, a sort of 4 cylinder Hornet. He lavished every care on it, no expense was spared when it came in for service and it shone like a new pin. One day he told me he wanted to sell it so I bought it to replace the Austin 7. We had two Alsatians in those days and they were very pleased at the idea, lots more room in the back and their own door; no longer did they have to climb over the front seats. For once I had succeeded in pleasing everybody.

It was a wonderful little car. It went to Scotland when I sold it and if it still exists and is ever for sale I would love to buy it back. CGK 80 are you still about?

Her next car was another Austin. A complete stranger came in to ask the cost of fitting a new back axle to an A30. When I gave him the price he was a bit shattered and said he would sooner sell it cheap, as it was. On enquiring why he needed an axle I was told there was a terrible vibration and he had been informed it was coming from the diff. This seemed a bit odd to me so, as it was a nice little car otherwise, I took a chance and bought it. Sure enough, when I put it on the hoist the trouble was obvious – some cuckoo had bolted the exhaust rigidly to the body with angle iron. About £2 on new flexible mountings and we had a lovely little A30.

Around 1958 we became Concessionaires for the Facel Vega and this car was to dominate my working life for the next six years. I hope to devote a complete chapter to the Facel later on but its significance here is the interesting cars taken in part exchange. One was a 200 SE Mercedes D.H.C. which, although not a sparkling performer, went well enough and was a nice car to drive.

I used it for some time. In those days Mercedes were not as common on the roads as they are today and there were few other German makes except the VW. Audi hadn't been born and there were no Opels over here. It probably sounds silly today when patriotism is at a pretty low ebb, but I remember being a bit self-conscious about using it on Armistice Day.

Another Facel part exchange was a TD21 Alvis. I got to like this car in

Opposite top: *The main claim to fame of this Mercedes 220 Coupé is that it was the property of Lionel Bart. The registration number LB4 gave it a certain notoriety and I certainly enjoyed driving it despite the fact that it was nothing to get very excited about; just a rather pleasant tourer.*

Opposite bottom: *There is no guarantee that a lover of Aston Martins would enjoy the 300SL Merc. This is a standard gull-wing without the "go-faster" bits and pieces used by illustrious owners including Rob Walker and Tommy Atkins. Nevertheless this was an immensely fast car with leach-like roadholding which didn't prevent it from being tiring on a long run. I found that I was faster from A to B in a DB2.*

spite of its rather heavy feel and used it until it was sold. Like most TD 21 Alvis, it leaked water into the car, which was its only real fault. I have one today and in two years it hasn't leaked, but that could be because I never take it out in the rain!

One car I did enjoy was a Lancia Flaminia. I delivered a Facel to somewhere in the Newcastle area, returning with the Flaminia. Never a Lancia fan, I was nevertheless captivated by this car. There was no single feature that was outstanding but it just felt absolutely right and I gave it up eventually with great reluctance.

We also took in one or two Bentleys. I wasn't all that keen on the post-war Bentleys in those days, perhaps if I had just viewed them as high class motor cars and disregarded the pre-war Bentley image I might have enjoyed them more. In later years I have come to terms with them and the six I have owned will be covered in a separate chapter.

Other cars that I used were Jaguars of all descriptions, a Sunbeam Alpine, Humber Snipe, various Rovers and a Ford Pilot. The latter, mundane as it may be, was a jolly good car. I remember once in the racing days John Heath was desperate for some parts on a Sunday which were in Birmingham and I volunteered to fetch them. The only car available was a Ford Pilot, so I set off in it after lunch. Despite a torrential thunderstorm which lasted over half an hour and reduced visibility to a matter of yards, I was back with them early evening. And there were no motorways either at the time.

Aston Martin had now produced the DB4, a completely new design. Neither engine, chassis or body bore any resemblance to the Mk 3 and it was also slightly bigger and more powerful. We received our demonstrator, VPA 4, and it proved a worthy companion to the Facel HK500 we also ran.

Between the two of them we covered most of the high performance market, Ferrari being the only serious competitor. I was more involved with the Facel at that time but Astons still had a special place in my heart and I thoroughly

Our first DB4 demonstrator. This was another superb Aston requiring a different driving technique from the DB2 with its revised suspension arrangements. It was a real Grand Touring car in every sense of the term and another masterpiece.

enjoyed the DB4. I had long since given up competitive motoring but remained in several clubs, including the Hants and Berks.

As I had competed regularly at Great Auclum and had access to glamorous cars, I was usually asked to open the course and did this for several years with the DB4, HK500 and a Facel Excellence. Although to speed up the hill was not part of the exercise the temptation to do so was irresistible, especially with the Aston, and the Club officials who were my passengers enjoyed it tremendously.

Here is a Facel Vega HK500 new in 1961 and later sold to the comedian Dave King. Standing next to the car is a real curiosity – a contemporary Formula 2 Emeryson; in fact the Works car driven in a few races that year by Mike Spence who is seen standing behind it pointing out its features. You can just make out the exhaust cambox of the Coventry Climax FPF engine with which this car was powered. The Emeryson and Facel Vega must have had approximately the same performance but the HK500 certainly did it in greater comfort.

The handling characteristics of the DB4 were different to those of its predecessors and it needed a different technique on the road. At the start of production the factory was still at Feltham and I remember taking a DB4 over one day for various rectifications. The Aston works were at the far side of the old Hanworth aerodrome. To reach it one came in the main gate off Feltham High Street and proceeded along a winding road skirting the edge of the field. This road was completely open for the whole of its length with only grass on either side and was an invitation for a good dice that could not be ignored. I had got it down to a fine art on the DB2 series cars, but when I tried it on the DB4 I lost it completely, ploughing up the grass for a considerable distance.

As it was within sight of the factory I was a bit embarrassed in case anyone had seen me, so when giving the repair instructions I asked them to look at the throttle, saying it had stuck on me as I came in. I never knew if they believed me but had a little chuckle to myself when I collected the car and was told the throttle had been rectified!

Another car we took up for a brief period was the Panhard, a revered old French make which was now part of the Citroën organisation. The car was called the PL17, and it bristled with technical innovations, but I thought it was a horrible little car. I collected the first one from Slough and ran it in but was glad to hand it over to one of the salesmen at 500 miles. We also had a short relationship with Renault. I used the Dauphine demonstrator for a while which wasn't a bad little car but I thought the 1100 we had later was much better.

In 1961 Hilda had her first new car, an Austin A40, it was a pleasant little car and although these days it is not regarded as highly as the Morris 1000, I liked it better at the time. Hilda liked it better too as the steering was lighter and, probably more important, the body shape hadn't been around for over ten years. In May 1962 we took it on an extended continental holiday starting with Norway, sailing from Newcastle and travelling overnight to Bergen. I had never been to Norway before and the plan was to press on to Oslo, staying a night en route if necessary. We landed about midday; ours was the only car, so although I was in the RAC, the AA man took us under his wing. He appeared horrified at my plan, saying motoring in Norway just wasn't that easy and we would never do it. He then suggested we go to a little place called Os, and that he could fix us up at the hotel.

After a succession of used cars I eventually bought this Austin A40 saloon for Hilda in 1961. Regrettably since this experience she has never been prepared to accept another used car. The A40 went on a holiday trip to Norway and various European countries proving an extremely comfortable little tourer.

I couldn't be certain whether he was genuine or on a rake-off from the hotel in question, but felt it would be wiser to give him the benefit of the doubt. It turned out to be a very sound decision. He was quite right, motoring in Norway wasn't that easy and, although not a great distance away, it took us twice as long to reach Os than a similar journey at home. Os was a delightful spot with only one hotel, the Solstrand, right on the edge of the fjord. It was first class, spotlessly clean, the people were charming and the food superlative. We liked it so much we stayed for three days. We did a bit of local touring and when we went back to Bergen to do some shopping I sought out my AA friend to suitably reward him.

We eventually left for Oslo; the hotel manager warned us that there would still be snow about and even advised me to put the car on the train, but I didn't reckon that. It was fascinating motoring; we hardly saw another car, at times the road was little more than a rough track and there were constant little detours to avoid fallen rocks. In due course we reached a little place on the edge of Hardanger fjord where the road ended and a small hand-operated ferry took us across to rejoin the road. I was staggered as it was marked on the map as the main road and I suppose, as the only route between Bergen and Oslo, it was. We reached Geilo in the evening, spending the night in a charming timber-built hotel. Amongst the few cars in the hotel car park was a UK-registered Humber, but we didn't meet the occupants. Heavy snow fell in the night but we set off and the road improved as we progressed until we reached a plateau where it became a cutting through high banks of snow. It lasted for several miles, just one car's width, with passing places hewn out of the snow every so often.

The snow piled on either side was about the height of a double decker bus and it was a weird sensation as driving between the two banks I couldn't keep the car straight. As we approached Oslo we entered another world; the change in climatic conditions was remarkable, almost as if a barrier had been lifted, the winter vanished and we were enjoying spring sunshine, leafy trees and flowers.

A few days in Oslo and we embarked on the Kronprins Harald for Kiel. It was a memorable trip and the ship was like a mini liner. We sailed down the Kattegat in brilliant sunshine and glistening with snow were the hills of Sweden on one side and Denmark on the other. Darkness came all too soon and we had a fabulous meal and retired to our cabin. We awoke to the sound of the quayside bustle at Kiel and, after surprisingly few formalities, set off for Hamburg, Bremen and the Dutch border.

We had one night in Germany and next morning headed for Delft where we stayed for a few days, exploring the delightful little town and using it as a base for trips to The Hague and other interesting places. Our hotel was first class, the only problem being I couldn't eat all the beautiful food they placed before us. I remember one evening when, having dined to capacity, the biggest bowl of strawberries and cream I've ever seen was set down in front of us. I have almost a passion for strawberries and cream and it broke my heart to admit defeat when about halfway through. Reluctantly we set off for Belgium, spent the night in Veurne, did some shopping in Ostend and then crossed the border into France, making for Le Touquet.

For some years I had been commuting regularly to Paris on Facel business, often collecting new cars, and usually managed to organise my schedule to give me a night in Le Touquet prior to catching an early flight next day.

When George Abecassis decided to retire from racing we built this HWM Jaguar Coupé from surplus parts. It looks as though the body was designed and built in Italy but in fact it was designed by Abecassis and built locally. It was a beautifully made car with a very sophisticated specification all mod cons and stupendous performance. The car was sold to Peter Palumbo, and I understand that it is still going strong and now resident in France.

If I had enough money left I would stay at the Chateau de Montreuil, about 18 km. from Le Touquet itself and it was towards this delectable spot that I pointed the nose of the little A40. We sampled their usual gastronomic delights, retired to a bedroom which was steeped in atmosphere with an uneven wooden floor and old oak beams, but mercifully modern plumbing. After a morning showing Hilda the town and walking along the magnificent beach we caught the Silver City air ferry to Lydd, arriving home in the evening. It was a wonderful trip and, in view of all we had done and seen, not outrageously expensive. After all, you can get through a lot of money just swanning around over here. The little A40 didn't miss a beat.

The DB4 gave way to the DB5, various mechanical improvements were made, the most significant being a change to smaller road wheels. The overall effect was to give more performance and much nicer handling. The body remained the same but the headlamps were now deeply recessed into the wings and faired in with moulded covers. I must admit I preferred the more aggressive frontal aspect of the DB4, but then I'm old-fashioned. In fact, my two nephews, who were well up with the phraseology of the day, used to say I wasn't even a square, I was a cube! I had some good runs in DB5s; they were great cars.

In the early sixties we took up Volvo and I ran the P1800 demonstrator. This was a jolly nice little car; quite nippy and comfortable. It handled well and would cruise happily in overdrive on a long run. Such was its stability that one day going through Camberley the chap behind started hooting and flashing his lights. At first I thought he was just in a hurry, but he persisted, so I stopped. He pointed to the rear wheels so I got out and found the near

During the period that we were agents for Volvo I ran this P1800; a type immortalised by Roger Moore in the "Saint" series. It was a very nice little car and today becoming a collectable rarity. While we were agents for Volvo we received a visit from the BMC man who told us we had either to give up Volvo or Wolseley. He got quite a shock when we gave up Wolseley. What would you have done?

side tyre was flat, but I hadn't felt a thing inside the car. I like a big engine on a long run but one day we had to make a trip to Penrith and the only car available was a Volvo saloon and I was pleasantly surprised at the way it covered the ground.

Another car I got involved in was the DAF. It was unknown over here but we were approached by the Dutch manufacturers who wanted us to become Concessionaires. We had recently formed a new company, Intercontinental Cars Ltd., to handle the Facel and taken large premises in Egham, so we had plenty of space. We were also clued-up on all the import rigmarole, having done it for some time with Facel and Iso Rivolta. The Sales Director, Tim Greenley, was keen on it so we had a go. It sold remarkably well. Tim, who was not at his best with cars like the Facel or the

Another pleasant car was this Lancia Flavia Coupé, fitted with a rather modest flat 4 push rod engine driving the front wheels. It was a car much more enjoyable on a long journey than when running about locally. When I delivered it to Scotland having sold it to a friend of mine there I felt I had at last found an ideal use for it. Sadly like so many Italian cars of the period the beautiful steel Pininfarina bodywork had limited life but it was lovely while it lasted.

Aston, really went to town on the little DAF and they were soon selling well. We had two demonstrators and if I had to go to London I never thought of using anything else. Mostly they came in by sea but some came by the Le Touquet – Lydd air ferry. One day I was at Lydd, having come from Paris, and was awaiting Customs clearance on some spares I had brought in. There were a number of DAFs on the tarmac and one of the bods started to move them into the bonded storage compound. He was giving them no end of stick, quite unnecessarily, so I went up to him.

They all knew me at Lydd, having brought in dozens of Facels, but didn't know I was anything to do with DAF, so he was very surprised to find

Another lovely Pininfarina bodied car is the Ferrari 250 GT series. This 2+2 example was a little more practical than most in that one adult or two children could be squeezed behind the front seats. It was a large car but adequately powered by the 3-litre V12 engine making all the right noises and sensations. I very much enjoyed it but like most Ferraris that I have driven I found the suspension rather harsh at slow speeds although once on the move it was superb.

himself on the wrong end of a jolly good rocket.

Eventually it got too big for us so a new company was formed, headed by Noel Cunningham Reid. They took over the old Aston works at Feltham and I assisted them to set up the Service Dept. and then baled out.

In 1964 production of the Facel came to an end. We continued to get the cars already in the pipeline – one of the last we sold to Ringo Starr – and for a time I was kept busy making almost weekly trips to Paris in our Morris 1000 Traveller, bringing back spare parts before they dried up. We sold the premises in Egham and once more I was back amongst the Jaguars and Astons. The DB6 came along, not as pretty as the DB5, but a good car nevertheless.

One high spot was the purchase of two DBR1s from the factory, both ex-Team cars. They were quite out of this world and the nearest thing to a road going Grand Prix car you would be likely to find. Driving them on the road was a bit tricky as they were not very tractable in traffic and the exhaust was too noisy to give them a blip of throttle. Once on the open road they were sheer poetry. They were driven in all the major sports car races and by all the top British drivers with the possible exception of Mike Hawthorn. Even Stirling, with all his experience of potent machinery, described them as superlative. I have no idea now where they went but I do remember how sorry I was to see them go. Looking back I suppose they must have been one of the last 'proper' racing sports cars, capable of being driven quite sensibly on the road as well.

Hilda's A40 had gone, to be replaced by an MG 1100. It was our first one, very smart in Old English White and Dark Green. This turned out to be a super little car and proved to be the first of many 1100s and 1300s she had. We took it twice to Guernsey, flying Silver City from Hurn. The first time I booked a passage for Bruno, our Alsatian, and reserved a box for him. He was a big dog even for an Alsatian and when they produced the box it was much too small, so they bent the rules and said he could travel in the car.

After her A40 Hilda ran a series of 1100/1300 BMC models. This is a plain Morris version which started life Old English White but at this stage had acquired a top painted in Facel Brunswick Blue. Her other cars of this type included MG, Austin GT and Riley versions and we always managed to dispose of them before the demon rust attacked. Registration number 77 PJ has passed down from car to car and now appears on Hilda's Honda Prelude.

The fun came when it was time to go aboard. As anyone who used Silver City in those days will remember, the cars had to be driven into the aircraft by their own staff. Not one of them would go near the MG with Bruno in the back, so they had to bend the rules again and let me drive it on. They were a really friendly crowd at Silver City. I hadn't used Hurn before but the chaps at Lydd and Le Touquet were a jolly good bunch. I must have made over a hundred trips. I still have a letter they wrote me when I had made over sixty and they said I was their most frequent passenger then. Naturally, I got to know them all, aircrew and ground staff, and it helped a lot as I could very seldom make a firm booking. Once, at Le Touquet, I was desperate to get home that evening; it was getting dark and they didn't fly passengers at night, but they were flying pigs. They suggested that if I didn't mind a pig plane they would get me across, but it was against all the rules as there would be no steward and it was a violation of Board of Trade regulations to fly me without one. I agreed to this so they called one over from Lydd and, having discharged its load of pigs, I went aboard. I think the car was described on the manifest as freight and I was a pig. The stench was appalling and hung around me for days in spite of several baths and clean clothes. But I got home and the episode was typical of the friendly relationship we had.

With the demise of Facel I found I had time on my hands and felt a bit like a lame duck. Nearly all my efforts over the previous six years had been devoted to Facel and, to a lesser extent, the Iso Rivolta. The Works Manager coped adequately with the Aston, Jaguar and BMC business whilst a new Sales Manager with Aston experience was able to demonstrate them. Obviously I was still in touch with it all and could do my bit to assist but could not get too stuck in without upsetting the others. As it was I sensed an atmosphere of, 'Now he's got nothing to do I suppose he will poke his nose into my job'. I didn't like this any more than I liked not having enough to do, neither was the situation helped by George Abecassis who seemed to resent that there were now two of us doing very little.

I thought the best thing to do was to opt out while we were all good friends and decided to look around for a small garage of my own. I wanted something not too far away, not only for my own convenience but because I was well known in the district and a lot of my friends promised to support me. It was about eighteen months before anything became available, when I was approached by Gulf Oil and offered the tenancy of a garage about half a mile from home. I formed a limited company, two of my old Facel customers became shareholders and I was in business.

I left H W Motors with many regrets, having spent all my working life at the same place, albeit under four different owners. I enjoyed the last twenty years with HWM and, although I felt I had contributed a lot to their success, I was also conscious of the fact that they had given me opportunities to widen my own experience which I would never had elsewhere. For that I was extremely grateful.

We had the traditional booze-up. Unbeknown to me the chaps had booked a room in one of the local pubs where they gave me a right Royal send off and some nice presents which I still have. A more formal lunch with George and the other Directors, bags of good wishes all round and I was ready for a new challenge.

I hope to write about the next twenty years but before doing so would like to re-cap a bit, cover the racing years and devote a little bit of space to various cars I either owned or became involved with.

5

PERSONAL REMINISCENCES OF EARLY POST-WAR RACING

The prospects for motor racing just after the war looked pretty bleak. We were in a state of austerity, petrol was rationed and of poor quality, Brooklands had gone, many of the pre-war cars had been destroyed and several well known drivers had been killed. In addition most people were occupied in getting back on their feet. Nevertheless, there was a determination to get started, cars were coming out of storage and suitable venues were being sought.

When I joined H W Motors I hoped we would get involved. George Abecassis was well known for his exploits before the war, notably at Crystal Palace, and I knew John Heath was keen. My hopes were soon realised and preparations began to race wherever possible.

Pre-war there were only three road circuits available for motor racing in Great Britain: the Mountain Circuit at Brooklands; Donington Park and Crystal Palace. During the war however numerous aerodromes had been constructed and many of these later became the basis for the modern racing circuits of our country. The first post-war event was held in 1947 at Gransden Lodge, a former bomber station and almost the entire motor racing fraternity turned out to celebrate the return of a beloved sport. Abecassis, who had been outstandingly successful in 1938/39 with this supercharged 1½-litre Alta came to Gransden with the car in its pre-war form and did extremely well driving under the wet conditions he enjoyed. It wasn't so easy to find petrol at this time but the real racers running on alcohol were able to obtain an appropriate diet and then burn it off with glee at every opportunity.

Before the war I had been a devotee of Brooklands since I was about 13 years old, had worked on competition cars and followed racing avidly. In those days it was a rich man's sport and as my own finances would have made the proverbial church mouse look like a millionaire, I could only hover about on the fringe. We all had ways and means of getting into Brooklands when we were kids and I was no exception, but I achieved great prestige amongst my mates through being spoken to by the legendary Malcolm Campbell. I didn't tell them that all he said was, "Get that bloody bike out of here!".

When I joined HWM we had an early ERA, the single seater Alta raced pre-war by Abecassis and a 2-litre Alta sports racing car. These were shortly joined by the 3.3 Bugatti mentioned earlier.

We started off with the ERA at Elstree where speed trials were held on the aerodrome runway. This was followed by circuit racing at Gransden Lodge, hill climbing at Prescott and Shelsey Walsh. We had reasonable success and it was all very encouraging. I acted as mechanic on these occasions, usually managing to drive the cars a bit in practice and testing sessions.

July 1946 saw our first International event, the Grand Prix des Nations at Geneva where several British drivers were taking part and George Abecassis entered the single seater Alta. Much feverish preparation went on, an ex-army Ford V8 truck was purchased to transport cars, spares, tyres, etc., everything was loaded up and we set off. Heath and Abecassis travelled in a Riley saloon with their wives and I followed on with the truck. We went via Folkestone and Ostend, heading for Brussels. The Riley pressed on ahead and I met up with them at the hotel. One of the porters knew of a garage about two kilometres away where the truck could be locked up for the night so he piloted me to it. Next morning he had gone off duty and no-one knew where to find him. I had only the vaguest idea where we had gone the previous night so it took about an hour to find the truck. Not a very auspicious start!

We had a leisurely run through Belgium and France – panic trips were to come later – staying the night in Reims. It was a depressing run, most of the towns had been destroyed either in the fighting or by the Germans as they retreated. The war had been over barely a year so not much had been done in the way of restoration. Nissen huts were in frequent use as shops, dwellings and even churches, standing amongst the piles of rubble. Words cannot describe our reactions when we reached Geneva. For years we had endured rationing, shortages, queues, etc., and suddenly we were in Fairyland, a veritable Aladdin's cave. The shops were full of everything, the people were well dressed and enjoying a way of life we had forgotten ever existed. The British were still heroes although Switzerland had not been involved in the war and we were treated like kings. They seemed convinced we were on the verge of starvation; in the hotel and in restaurants the most delicious food was piled on the table in enormous quantities.

We had a day in which to soak this up and then the practice sessions began. It meant getting up at the crack of dawn as they could only close the roads for a short period in the early morning. Great Britain was

represented by Raymond Mays, Bob Gerard, Prince Bira, Peter Whitehead, Leslie Brooke and Geoff Bainbridge on ERAs, Abecassis in the Alta, Reg Parnell with a Maserati and David Hampshire in the faithful old Delage. The cars were all pre-war, even Reg's Maserati, but he was really the only Englishman in with a chance. With continental drivers like Nuvolari, Trossi, Varzi, Wimille and Farina all mounted on either the latest Maserati or the beautiful Tipo 158 Alfa-Romeo, our chaps were just in it for the ride. Looking after us all and representing the RAC was Earl Howe, veteran racing driver, diplomat, ace organiser and a genius at sorting out problems, great or small. He had an immaculate Type 57S Bugatti finished in his colours of blue and black. It had to be towed to start every morning, apparently the normal procedure. I remember thinking, magnificent car though it was, I couldn't have put up with that. Much as I like fiddling about with cars I am very much a 'get in and press the button' type of motorist where my everyday transport is concerned. We were all allocated a garage to use as a base and ours was a spotless little service station near the centre of the town. The practice sessions were taken dead seriously and we worked hard. Plugs, carburettor settings, ignition timing, etc., were all changed a dozen times to get the best combination. We had continuous trouble with a locking front brake on the Alta and one stalwart changed his diff, three times to get the best axle ratio.

My great moment came on the eve of the race when, after practice, scrutineering took place at a point halfway round the course. After it was over the mechanics drove the cars back to the paddock and believe me it was some dice. If the drivers could have seen us once we disappeared round the first corner they would have rated their chances of appearing on the grid next day as pretty small.

Opposite left: *Abecassis entered the Grand Prix des Nations in Geneva in 1946; a race for which a magnificent selection of Formula One machinery and drivers turned up. Apart from experiencing life as we could hardly remember it in neutral Switzerland, we were reminded of the glamour of those pre-war days by the inclusion of examples of the finest racing cars extant in 1939 and which had survived the hostilities. To mark the importance of the occasion Abecassis completely rebuilt his Alta from the form in which it was seen earlier at Gransden and it will be noted that the body now has a lower tail and new coat of paint although the majority of the mechanical elements were exactly in pre-war form. On the occasions when I drove this car I found it extremely fast but rather skittish; thanks to the virtually non-existent suspension system resulting from the use of Lancia-like sliding pillars front and rear which really only had a practical up and down movement of a couple of inches. This was a very rudimentary form of independent suspension which presented few advantages over the classical cart sprung systems used by ERA and others.*

Opposite bottom: *Arguments rage over who was the greatest driver of any era but few will quarrel with the award to Tazio Nuvolari of that title for the Thirties. His drives against and at the wheel of German 750 kg. cars are legendary. By the post-war period Nuvolari was suffering from a weak chest and was seriously affected by the fumes of racing fuel although that is not a mask but a rain visor that he is wearing here. His post-war performances were never as overwhelmingly superior as hitherto but still demonstrated flashes of his earlier brilliance. Nuvolari is driving a Works 4CL Maserati fitted with two-stage supercharged 4-cylinder 16-valve engine of $1\frac{1}{2}$ litre capacity. On this occasion even Nuvolari's genius could not resist the domination of the Works Alfa Romeos.*

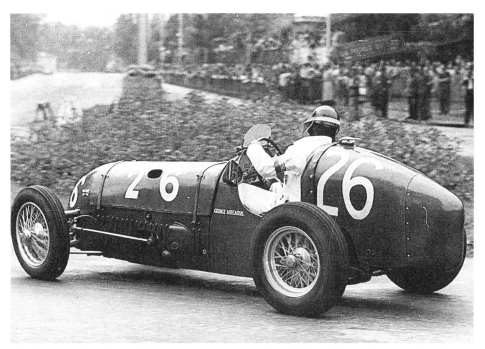

Another excellent shot of Abecassis at Geneva in the 1½ litre Alta with modified and lowered tail section. Altas were manufactured by the remarkable Geoffrey Taylor at Kingston, using empirical methods. It is said that Taylor never bothered with engineering drawings but got on with making his engines and cars while modifying them in the light of experience; no two ever being the same. With about a dozen employees at most Taylor continued to produce not only cars of his own invention but supplied power units and other components to contemporary British Racing Car manufacturers including us at HWM and Connaught among others. I often felt that if a bit more support had been given to Taylor rather than to BRM we might have got further, faster

In the evenings we went on the town. Geneva was full of the carnival spirit, the bars were packed with excited people, anyone connected with the race was feted and plied with drinks. The glamour of it all attracted the most gorgeous females, we all did ourselves very well, and more than one driver regretted the lack of foresight which had prompted him to bring his wife!

The day of the race dawned cold and wet, just like home. It was to be run in two heats and a final. George was in the second heat and for a long time lay third. The challenge of the Italian cars was too great for this to last and he finished a very creditable sixth, thus qualifying for the final. At the end of the heat we found the petrol tank was split. There were no facilities for repairing it in the pits so the authorities, strictly against the rules, let us take the car back to our garage. When the proprietor learned we were going to put an acetylene torch on a tank that was barely drained of highly volatile racing fuel his face paled and he lit off down the road to watch his garage blow up from a safe distance. The repair went smoothly; I steadied the tank and turned it as John wielded the torch and it was not until afterwards that we confessed to each other how frightened we had been.

A view of de Graffenried in a Maserati 4CL leading Abecassis in the Alta and Wimille in the Tipo 158 again at Geneva for that wonderful visit to Paradise that we made in 1946. The other Alfa Romeos are out of sight in a race in which everyone else was very much "also-ran".

The final was a walkover for the Italians but Bira did manage sixth place in his ERA. We had another good session that night and next day I set off home in the truck, the rest of the party staying on for a few days. It was arranged I should give a lift to a middle-aged Swiss character, the idea being that I dropped him off as near to Paris as my route took me. Once on the road I got thinking I wouldn't mind going to Paris myself so I struck a bargain with him. I would take him all the way if he would pay for the extra petrol and help me get some more coupons. He was quite happy about this so off we went. My Swiss friend knew Paris well so we were soon fixed up with a meal and a bed and next day went to the Bureau d'Essence for some more coupons.

My companion went in. What he had told them I do not know, but he came out with a big wad of coupons. I then had the idea that perhaps the officials might not connect a fluent French speaking Swiss with a gormless Englishman so I went in as well. I told them that due to the poor French signposting I had lost my way and really should have been in Reims instead of Paris and was running out of coupons. It seemed to work and I too got a wad. I was all for getting out smartly but my pal knew the form. The office was on a sort of landing with several doors leading off it and one or two seats. We pooled the two lots of coupons, worked out how many I would need and added a few for emergencies. He then crossed the landing to some bods sitting on the seats and flogged the rest of them. I couldn't believe it – there was a black market in petrol coupons at home but it didn't operate outside the door of the Petroleum Office! I really couldn't get out fast enough then, but there was no problem. We split the money and I set off for Ostend.

For the GP des Nations at Geneva in 1946 Alfa Romeo entered four of their Tipo 158 Grand Prix cars which completely dominated the race. They were driven by Farina (the winner), Varzi (7th), Trossi (2nd) and Wimille (3rd). All four cars had been constructed at the outbreak of war for the 1940 Tripoli GP and although two of the four cars were even further modified from that form here is Wimille driving his 158 in perhaps the purest form – with single stage supercharging and enough power to make it a difficult machine for all but the most experienced of drivers; particularly in the rain as here. Every time I look at this picture I confirm my personal rating of "most beautiful racing car ever" and enjoy the clear view of the driver at work

I had a good run until very near Ostend when, after a fair old belt along one of the excellent roads built by the Germans during the war, there was a terrific bang from the rear. Pulling up to investigate I found the off-side tyre in ribbons, although it hadn't deflated. It was a monumental task to change it as the spare was in the back along with all the racing equipment, churns of fuel, etc., and I had to shift most of the stuff to get the spare wheel out. Changing it was no light task either. It was a hot day and I was exhausted by the time I had finished.

Just outside the town I saw a café, stopped and went in. Before I could say a word the fellow behind the bar said, "You look as if you could do with a pint, mate". He was an ex-British soldier who had married a Belgian

I make no excuses for including another shot of the ex-Charlie Martin Type 59 "Bug". It has to be one of the most beautiful cars of all time and although it did not achieve many successes against contemporary opposition, it remains my favourite Bugatti. Here the car is in hill climb form at Prescott complete with the twin rear wheels used at that time for sprints.

After the war the market was flooded with surplus army vehicles which were hungrily snapped up and pressed into civilian use. We bought this Ford V8 truck and used it as our racing car transporter. It was a thirsty brute – the sidevalve V8 being not particularly efficient – but it was a reliable racing car transporter, shown here crossing France en route for Geneva in 1946; hardly more than a year since it might have been crossing the same terrain in anger.

girl and settled there. He was dead right about the pint – it went down in one great swig! I stayed the night with him but my troubles were not quite over, for next morning I found the spare I had fitted was flat. A local garage changed the inner tube with the one from the damaged tyre, but the delay caused me to miss the boat. The next one out had no space for the truck so, as I had run out of money, I left it with the RAC for shipment on the first available ferry. About a week later I picked it up from Folkestone and, much to my surprise, everything was still inside.

The rest of 1946 was uneventful, George Abecassis took the Bugatti to Shelsley in October but I did not go with him. During the winter preparations were made for a much busier season in 1947 and the stable was joined by ERA R2A. This car had been modified before the war by owner Embiricos to take Tecnautoi IFS and had a cowl fitted over the radiator, giving it a more modern appearance.

The first race with this car was the Swedish Winter Grand Prix held on a snow-packed aerodrome at Rommehed. This trip was to last two or three weeks so I could not go. There were two other ERA's driven by Reg Parnell and Leslie Brooke. They raced as a team, finishing in team order with Abecassis in third place. There was another meeting near Stockholm, this time on a frozen lake, and George was second. Next came the International meeting in Jersey but our car was unplaced.

Our original blown 2-litre Alta sports car was still with us but for racing John Heath bought a more potent one, EOY 8, destined to be well known before the year was out. He took it to Chimay at the end of May, coming in a highly commendable second in the unlimited sports car race.

Various home meetings had come and gone. I managed to get to most of them but was unable to go to Ulster where George Abecassis again took third place in the ERA. The next big meeting was in the Isle of Man.

Seen outside HWM with my first competition car, a lovely little Riley Nine bought in 1947. KV 9475 was later sold to an airline pilot who ran it for some time and then it was eventually bought by Leslie Hawthorn for his son Mike to begin his racing career. He made it go a lot faster than I did!

If you had my good fortune you would have been smiling too at the wheel of EJJ 703 which we sold to Tony Gaze the Australian Alta-fancier who after this 2 litre owned a succession of cars of the type which he campaigned successfully in Europe and later in Australia. We were sorry to see this original Alta go but of course we had a replacement in EOY 8. The snap was taken by my pal who had followed in my Ford Prefect as a tender. We took a breather here at Seven Springs, Gloucester

Abecassis again took the ERA and drove a magnificent race, leading for about quarter distance until a bad oil leak slowed him down, finally causing him to have a minor shunt when oil sprayed over the pedals and on to his goggles.

Before 1947 was out I was to have my first taste of competition motoring. During the summer we had purchased a Riley 9 Ulster, a very nice little car and reputed to have been one of the works team cars pre-war. I managed to persuade John Heath to let me enter it in the Brighton Speed Trial. I knew it would stand no chance as it was much too heavy for a sprint car and the pre-selector gearbox absorbed far too much of the power developed by the little 1089cc engine, but it would be fun.

However, the week before Brighton we were at Prescott with two cars including the 2-litre Alta which John Heath drove in the sports car class.

After the meeting he felt like a more civilised journey home and asked if I would take the Alta back to Walton. Naturally I agreed so off he went with Abecassis in his car. I had a little unfinished business to attend to in the beer tent and left about half an hour afterwards. About halfway home I came upon them sitting by the roadside drinking coffee. Of course I stopped to see if they were in trouble and on being assured that all was well I set off again. I suppose I wanted to show off a bit so made a good clean racing start and shot up the road with some nice crisp gearchanges. The next day John called me up to his office. He said, "Now Fred, George and I watched you yesterday when you took off in the Alta". He went on, "I have to go away next weekend and will not be able to drive it at Brighton and we both think you can handle it well enough to drive it for me. Would you like to do it?". Would I like to! He had to be joking. The Riley might be fun but with the Alta I was in with a chance.

Although officially a sports car it was, in fact, a thinly disguised racing car. It weighed very little and the supercharged 2-litre engine gave it tremendous power low down combined with a three figure top speed. This,

Don't be deceived by my casual appearance at Brighton. The Alta required a lot of concentration to drive fast and I was more worried than I looked.

of course, in the days when very few road cars would reach 100 mph.

When the day came I had my two runs in the Riley and shortly afterwards found myself on the line with the Alta. All went well and I recorded a time of 32.20 seconds, giving me third fastest sports car time of the day, being beaten into 2nd place by 0.25 seconds and first place by 0.60 seconds, very little in it and both the other cars of higher capacity. Well pleased with myself I returned home wondering how I could manage a few drives the following year. It was obviously not going to be easy, the Riley was being sold and I knew John had a full programme for the Alta. Then fate dealt kindly with me again.

The partners heard of an MG K3 Magnette for sale near Edinburgh and bought it without seeing it. When it arrived they were shattered; it was a really dejected looking heap and I could see they were in a quandary. It needed a complete rebuild and various parts were missing, the supercharger had been removed and lay in pieces in a box, minus its drive shaft. With their racing commitments there was no way they could do it and it was not a job for the ordinary workshop which had to earn money anyway.

I had my eye on this but, before anything could be done about it, John Heath and I went to Lausanne with the ERA. It was an International meeting with a race for cars up to 1100 cc, followed by a Formula One Grand Prix over 90 laps of the 2 mile circuit. John had entered for the Grand Prix; it was his first major continental event and I think he was glad of my moral support apart from the assistance I was able to give him. Everything was loaded into the faithful old Ford truck and I set off. John flew over and we met up in Paris, where we stayed the night. We made an early start the next day and, taking it in turns to drive, we were able to press on, reaching

Here I am enjoying the 2 litre Alta at Brighton and holding off a rather positive-cambered Allard in the process. The supercharged 2 litre had superb performance for its time and gave me a third in class and third FTD for Sports Cars in the 1947 Speed Trials. I drove the car down to the coast from Walton and took my current girlfriend in the passenger seat. After a particularly "hairy" stretch on the road down I turned to ask how she liked it only to find that she had completely passed out. This was probably the only time I got a girl worried while we were still moving!

A side view of ERA R2A showing the modified cowl as it stands in the HWM forecourt. This was the car that John Heath and I took to Lausanne.

Lausanne late in the evening.

The British contingent consisted of John Heath, Peter Whitehead, David Hampshire, all on ERAs and Reg Parnell with a 4CLT Maserati. This was one of the Scuderia Milan cars but it was pretty obvious the Italians had no intention of letting Reg beat their own drivers. The car was badly prepared and only had a single stage blower whereas he has been promised a two stage one.

Once more our cars were no match for the continentals. The Maseratis were joined by two 4.5-litre Talbots driven by Chiron and Giraud-Cabantous and the poor old ERAs didn't get a look in.

Here is a fine action photo of Peter Whitehead at speed in the "country" section of the course at Lausanne in 1947. The car is ERA R10B, purchased new by Whitehead in 1936. Today it is raced in VSCC events by Nick Mason.

John Heath is blowing smoke in my eyes and having a little chat to discuss tactics at Lausanne in 1947. The car is ERA R2A which had been fitted in 1937 with Tecnauto independent front suspension by its first private owner, Embiricos. The non-standard radiator cowl didn't do very much for the car's appearance or speed but in fact considering this was John Heath's first Grand Prix he did very well; finishing 7th

The pace was fast and furious with Ascari leading at first, but he retired with brake trouble letting Villoresi into the lead, a position he held to the end. Surprise of the race was the speed of the little unsupercharged Simca. Although outwardly the same as the 1100 cc cars that had finished first and second in the earlier race, it had been bored out to 1220 cc and in the hands of Jean Pierre Wimille was really motoring.

Poor Reg was soon in trouble with brakes and steering and, retiring early in the race, proceeded to help the rest of us in the pits. About halfway through John Heath came in saying he had hit the curb and his steering felt funny. Now Reg was an expert at shunting ERAs and knew the form. In a flash he had removed the drop arm from the steering box to reveal a sheared key. He had a spare in his box so whilst he got it I removed the broken pieces, the new key was fitted, and drop arm put back and John was away in a total time of 3.5 minutes. He finished well down the field but was happy to have finished at all in his first major Formula One race.

The evening celebrations followed the usual pattern and our party was soon joined by a dark-haired floozy who attached herself firmly to us. She was what these days would be called a dolly bird and we immediately christened her Bostik because her eyelashes were thickly coated with black goo!

A riotous evening ensued but eventually it was time to go and we set off to stagger back to our hotel. We came to some roadworks and spotted a wheelbarrow. Peter Whitehead's mechanics grabbed it and suggested we give

Heath and Abecassis bought a second blown 2-litre Alta EOY 8 to run with their original car EJJ 703. Heath in particular was attached to his Altas and these particular models were the best made pre-war with shattering performance even with the supercharger removed. Here John Heath drives the 2-litre car unblown at Chimay; putting up a very good show. John never claimed to be a top line driver but was extremely consistent.

each other rides. This seemed a good idea so Bostik and I climbed in, the others seized the handles and off we went.

Our progress was a bit erratic and very noisy but all went well until the wheel got in a tram line, the barrow upended pinning me underneath, Bostik being thrown clear and landing in the road with her legs in the air. My mates stood there transfixed, so bemused by the sight of long stockinged legs, bare thighs, suspenders and little white panties that my feeble cries for help went unheard. Just then an 1100 cc Fiat pulled up with a squeal of brakes and out stepped two Swiss policemen. They stood there long enough to get a good eyeful themselves and then moved in to sort us out. They turned out to be a couple of good blokes and, having squared us up, escorted us back to our hotel, something it is doubtful we could have managed on our own.

What became of the floozy I never found out but I wouldn't think she ever realised how near she came to being ravished on an upturned wheelbarrow in the middle of Lausanne's main street.

Long before the drive-on ferry was invented our racing transporter had to be winched on board. Here it is being winched up with the tail of the ERA just showing on its way back from the Continent. John Heath was having kittens as he watched; wondering whether the contraband hidden away would be revealed if the vehicle should crash to the ground . . .

Here is the Riley lined up on the pavement at the Marina Drive, Brighton, for my first competition drive there. Although it was a beautiful little car the Riley was rather heavy and not particularly powerful and on this occasion was too slow to win any prizes.

The Riley in action at Brighton. Although acceleration was never its strong point I am glad to say that I did eventually catch and overtake the Austin "Nippy" seen apparently pulling away from me here. **5/16**

The next day we packed up to come home. I remember I felt pretty rough, especially when I bent down to pick something up. John Heath, having found himself something a bit more permanent to play with, decided to stay on for a while and fly home, so I set off on my own with the truck. I met up with Whitehead's boys again in Boulogne but by this time we had all run out of money so the celebrations were of the 'one glass of beer and three straws' variety.

This was to be my last trip of this sort as, when next year came round, the programme was much more extensive and needed a full-time mechanic. The ordinary garage side was also expanding and I could no longer afford to drop everything and take off.

The MG was still very forlorn in a corner of the workshop, so I approached John and George with a proposition. I would rebuild it in my own time if they would pay for the parts and let me race it when it was finished. They agreed without hesitation and that same night I came back after my evening meal and began what was going to be months of hard work.

The car was one of the few built with a pointed tail. The tail was in fact formed by the petrol tank, mounted separately from the body by cables, with a capacity of 27 gallons. These cars were all built for racing, the flat tank models being sold to the general public. They were raced in the Mille Miglia, all the major Brooklands races, the Mannin Beg in the Isle of Man, the Tourist Trophy etc. Drivers like Earl Howe, Birkin, Eyston, Nuvolari, Charlie Martin, Kaye Don etc. had all scored victories with them, and the thought that one of these famous backsides had sat in my seat was an extra incentive for me.

I began by stripping out to the bare frame. This was a sketchy affair and all the rivets had worked loose, so my first job was to line the frame up, weld all the rivets to the various cross members etc, and then weld them to the frame. This was much more satisfactory than drilling and re-rivetting and took far less time. Front and rear axles were then overhauled and refitted, brakes relined and the beautiful 13″ Elektron drums and back plates highly polished. Whilst this was going on the wheels were at a specialists, the front ones being re-spoked and the rears rebuilt to 16″ diameter with wide rims. They were then stove enamelled silver and some spare racing tyres fitted.

With the frame and axles sprayed green and its silver wheels and the polished drums shining through the spokes, it looked like a picture and I felt I was getting somewhere.

Meanwhile the body was at the coachbuilders. At some time an attempt had been made to lower the overall height by cutting a section out of the middle. The effect was good but the mod has been crudely carried out, so I had it properly done and the body tidied up generally. The radiator was at Serk being lowered to confirm with the new body height but increased in depth to give the same cooling area. As the exhaust ran along the outside of the body it had to be altered as well, so I got the redoubtable Les Anstead of Brooklands silencer fame to make me a new one.

A then stripped the engine and found it in remarkably good shape. With very little bore and piston wear, new rings would suffice and the valves were also very good, but I did fit new springs.

At that time I did a fair amount of business with a small firm called Brooklands Engineering. As their name implied, they had been at Brooklands before the war but, as their premises had been taken over by Vickers during the war, they were now at Cobham. They were extremely competent precision engineers, had always been involved in the racing game and turned out some beautiful work. They were also the manufacturers of Martlet racing pistons.

One day I was there talking to Charles Bray, who ran the place, when

A wonderfully atmospheric picture of John Heath bareheaded driving EOY 8 at Prescott on a sunny day. I drove the car back to Walton and then got my chance to drive it in the Brighton Speed Trials.

Here is a mouthwatering selection of machinery photographed in the HWM Showroom during 1947. On the left a 6C 1½-litre Maserati; a car I remember as a beautiful piece of machinery with wonderful handling and performance. My Riley Nine in the centre is flanked on the other side by a 2.3 Alfa. This little group would be worth a few pounds today and even then was rather expensive merchandise.

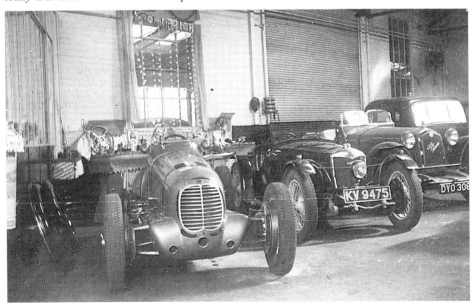

my eye caught sight of a crankshaft in the corner of his office. This was no ordinary crankshaft, but a highly polished breath-taking work of art. Whilst admiring the sheer perfection of it the shape suddenly looked familiar. I turned to old Bray and said, "That looks very much like a K3 Magnette crank". He replied, "It is, we had it specially made for a record breaking car but it was never used". He then went on to say, "That crank will go up to 7600 rpm."

This was incredible. Normally anything over 6500 rpm on a K3 could result in very expensive noises, but old Bray was a talented engineer and as straight as a die. If he said it would do 7600 then it would. I told him of my project and he said I could have it for £100. In 1947 £100 was a lot of money and I could not in all fairness expect Heath and Abecassis to pay for it, but I was determined to have it and decided to ask them if they would pay half if I did the same.

When I got back, John Heath was there, so I told him about this lovely crankshaft I could buy for £100. With no hesitation he replied. "Well Fred, you had better go back and get it". In less time than it takes me to write this I was in the secretary's office drawing a cheque and on my way back to Cobham. I kept it in my office until I was ready, right where I could sit and look at it. I dusted it every day and locked it up at night. Even now, when I see an antique expert drooling over a beautiful piece of furniture I know how he feels.

I overhauled and reassembled the supercharger and then had another bit luck. In nearby Weybridge was a garage with a little machine shop run by Frank Kennington who also raced a K3. It transpired he had at one time suffered a broken blower drive shaft and had made one, using the broken shaft as a pattern. He still had some of the special steel, the dimensions and a broaching tool for the splines. On hearing that mine was missing he offered to make me one and a beautiful job it was too.

Before assembling the engine I had to make sure the rest of it would stand 7000 rpm. I had all the bearings re-metalled to suit the new crank, had the flywheel balanced and then set about the con. rods. I went over each one with a fine needle file, removing any burr or blemish that could start

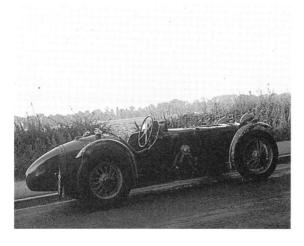

To replace the Riley Nine HWM acquired this rough supercharged K3 MG Magnette; the body of which had been lowered by an earlier owner. It needed a total rebuild which began almost immediately after purchase. It was driven down from Scotland but in fact it was in a much sorrier state than this snap suggests.

John Heath, cigarette in mouth, stands behind EOY 8, the supercharged 2-litre Alta which he continued to race after selling the original car to Tony Gaze. This photograph was taken at Prescott but the car was campaigned regularly in Hill Climbs, Sprints and circuit races at home and on the Continent.

a fatigue crack and they were then highly polished and balanced. Both pistons and rods were then weighed and sorted out to ensure each assembly was of equal weight to within very fine limits.

With the engine assembled and in the chassis, the radiator on, new throttle rods and levers made by hand and fitted, the time came to see if it would run. I connected up a temporary oil gauge, stuck the petrol pipe into a tin of fuel, fitted a slave battery and pressed the button. With a roar it burst into life, the oil gauge needle shot round the dial and, as it was well past midnight, I switched off in deference to the neighbours and went home highly delighted.

By this time we were well into 1948 and I had entered for the first Prescott meeting on Sunday, June 13th. There was still a lot of work to do and I worked every evening, but it was not until the Friday night before that I was ready for a road test.

The car was still unfinished but everything essential was there, so I went off to try it after work. Abecassis came with me as he had become more interested in the project as it came nearer to completion. He could raise very little enthusiasm for a load of bits scattered all over the garage floor, but the completed car was another matter and he was of great help to me during that evening's testing.

The first new car in my life was this 1947 Ford Prefect. I apologise for its inclusion in the racing chapter but my excuse is that it was used in all competitions for which it was suited. In this shot it is in use in driving tests organised by the Hants and Berks Motorclub.

We went out to a straight stretch of derestricted road about a mile away and belted up and down it for over an hour, changing carburetter needles, timing settings, etc., until the car felt right. It seems incredible that the same piece of road is now subject to a speed limit and full of traffic. It is doubtful if you could get up to 40 mph until late at night and then you would probably get nicked.

Satisfied, I went back to the garage, filled a spray gun with green paint, sprayed everything to cover up all the welds etc and went home. Next day, rather ashamed of its scruffy asppearance, I set off for Prescott with one of my pals following up in my car with all the tools and odd bits. The MG felt absolutely right, lively, tight as a drum and by the time I got there it had settled down nicely.

Practice that day was fun and very rewarding; nothing had to be touched on the car, the 110 mile drive from home had given me a chance to get used to it and I was ready for the big moment. I had friends in Upton St. Leonards about 18–20 miles away and we stayed the night with them so were able to be at the hill nice and early. I had the usual two run ups the hill and was highly delighted to finish 2nd in my class. First place was taken by Lionel Leonard, also in an MG. His car was a lightweight model based on the N-type chassis but with a blower which was very fast and he drove it beautifully. I never did manage to beat him. On arrival home I set to and finished the car off. It was then professionally painted in light metallic green, the colour later adopted for the HWM. It looked a picture and as there was no further mechanical work necessary I looked around for some more events to compete in. In the meantime our original 2-litre Alta sports car had been bought by Tony Gaze. I had a marvellous run delivering it to him at Ross-on-Wye, a friend following up in my Ford Prefect to bring me back. Although not as potent as EOY 8, it was still a very fast car with handling to match and I really enjoyed myself.

We had also started on constructing our own cars, the first one being

Opposite top: *The Prefect was ideal for driving tests, in which its 3-speed gearbox enabled one to make rapid changes in direction by the simple expedient of locking the back wheels while travelling forward at the same time engaging reverse, ready for the immediate "off". Provided you didn't tip it over, the Prefect was also very manoeuvrable and, at speeds up to 40 miles an hour, quite nippy.*

Opposite bottom: *Here is my K3 after a complete strip and rebuild in my spare time. It was a runner despite being unfinished and is here caught in the Prescott paddock next to Lionel Leonard's modified MG to the left.*

a modified Alta fitted with an all-enveloping two seater body. I went on the initial tests which were carried out on the RAF station at Odiham. The CO was a keen motor racing type and let us use the runways when it didn't

A view of the K3 coming off the banking at Great Auclum and showing to advantage the complex "octagonal" cowling of the blower which was driven at engine speed from the nose of the crankshaft.

Heath and Abecassis were very pleased with the performance of the two 2 litre supercharged Altas that they campaigned immediately after the war. However, some of the sports racing machinery in use on the continent was technically more advanced; particularly in the area of bodywork. They therefore set about converting a third Alta for serious competition in the sports racing class by removing the blower, carrying out sundry chassis modifications and

fitting a full width streamline body. This photograph was taken at RAF Odiham where the initial testing was carried out. John Heath and others are pushing while George takes the wheel.

interfere with flying. The tests were very satisfactory and, with a few adjustments, it was ready for racing. But before that Abecassis was to have a minor shunt on the Kingston By-Pass.

Apparently an old boy emerged from a side turning giving him no chance. Mind you he was no doubt shifting a bit. In the old chap's own words, "I stopped and looked up the road, there was nothing coming so I pulled out, then this thing appeared from nowhere and hit me".

The Alta had a chequered racing career. John Heath retired at Jersey with a broken timing chain, George Abecassis skidded into a ditch in the Spa 24 hour race and it shed a wheel in the Paris 12 hour race at Montlhéry,

By the time that I entered for Great Auclum I had completed the rebuild and look very pleased with myself. This car eventually was sold to the USA and is apparently still there, although rarely seen.

The K3 on the final stretch at Great Auclum. This was one of the friendliest venues and the course seemed ideally suited to the MG.

fortunately without serious results. However, it was all good experience. Talking of testing, when we first started after the war we used to get up at dawn and take the cars on to the A3 Portsmouth Road. It was quite something to see a single seater GP car hurtle over the rise near Wisley and bear down flat out to the junction at Paines Hill. It was all highly illegal but although the police must have known about it they turned a blind eye. The only trouble we had was with the Head at a nearby boy's school; apparently the noise would awaken the boys who would then hurriedly dress and come out to watch. Things certainly were different then!

I had for some years been a member of the JCC, subsequently to become the BARC, and in the early part of the year they announced that, by courtesy of the Duke of Richmond and Gordon, (himself a pre-war racing driver as the Earl of March), the Club would develop the Westhampnett Airfield as what came to be known as the Goodwood racing circuit. It was also

A second picture of the "new look" Alta which was very much John Heath's idea (he was always the engineer of the team). This photograph was taken at Goodwood after we had sold it on, following entry into the serious business of the HWM Motor Racing operation. It was quite a bit heavier than the "normal" Alta but the well streamlined coachwork gave it an advantage on fast circuits.

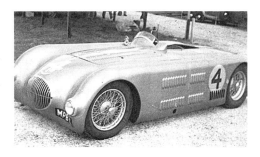

The first meeting at Goodwood circuit was held on 18 September 1948 and like many others I rushed to join in. For reasons which I cannot remember I entered the K3 less road equipment in a racing car class and you can see here the motley entry characteristic of the time which includes at the rear the Dunham Alvis (No. 35) and to the right of it the famous Rover Special now owned by Frank Lockhart, in its earliest form. This shot is taken at Madgwick corner and by the following year a safety ditch and bank had been constructed to protect the huge standing crowd.

announced that for a nominal sum, members could use it for testing. I booked it for a day, taking the K3 with one of my mechanics as a reward for some help he had given me on the car. It turned out a filthy wet day and we got soaked. I decided to have a go in spite of the weather. We were the only nutcases there, which I was quite happy about until, on what was later named the Lavant straight, I hit a patch of thick mud deposited by one of the farm tractors. I immediately spun several times and went off the road, the one thought in my mind being I must not overturn with no-one there to assist me. My mechanic was at the other side of the track and couldn't have done much on his own anyway. Fortunately I came to rest without any harm, but immediately packed up and never again practiced or tested without the proper facilities being available.

I ran the MG throughout the season, entering for Great Auclum, several minor club meetings, one or two Prescotts and the Brighton Speed Trials, being placed in most of the events and never far behind in the others. In September Goodwood officially opened with a full programme, a mixture of scratch and handicap races on the lines of the pre-war Brooklands meetings. For this meeting I removed the wings, lamps and other sports car features and ran it in the racing class, entering for two races, a scratch and a handicap. It was my first attempt at circuit racing and I thought it was great, especially the start of the scratch race, where the experience I had gained in sprints during the summer helped a lot. I was not placed in either event but was sufficiently high in the results to feel pleased with my first effort.

All good things must come to an end and, during the winter, I was to lose the MG. The consistent performance of the car and its immaculate appearance had attracted a lot of attention during the season and several people wanted to buy it. Business is business, so I could not blame the two partners for accepting a very good offer from a fellow named Johnson who lived in Peterborough.

Early in 1948 we had purchased two 6 C Maseratis, beautiful cars in the traditional Italian red with $1\frac{1}{2}$-litre 6-cylinder twin cam engines and single stage supercharging.

George Abecassis took one to Jersey in April, coming in 2nd to Bob Gerard's ERA. I managed to get a short drive in one of them and it was superb. One or two had a go in them and I have a strong feeling Duncan Hamilton was one but could be wrong after all this time. They were both sold to aspiring amateur racing drivers. Buster Baring, a builder from the Bracknell area bought one, the other went to Sam Gilbey who I think was connected with the well-known port wine concern. To the best of my recollection they had a lot more fun than success, but I'm sure they didn't mind that. On one occasion they were placed one behind the other on the grid. At the fall of the flag the front one stalled, the one behind promptly climbing up his tail.

Another car we bought was the single seater off-set blown Rapier, a pre war Brooklands outer circuit car raced before the war by Roy Eccles and post-war by Ian Metcalf. As I had managed to get through the 1948 season without any dramas, the two partners agreed to let me race this car during 1949, so during the winter months I got it ready.

There was little to do mechanically as it was in good order, but the car had been built for Brooklands, the steering and suspension having been set up to cope with a steep banking and for races run in an anti-clockwise direction. This was quite different from running clockwise on a flat aerodrome circuit with lots of corners and I knew Ian had found it a bit of a handful.

There was not much I could do about it without reconstruction, but I lowered the rear suspension, fitted 16" wheels on the rear with wider tyres and experimented with different damper settings. Hopefully, I entered it for the Easter Monday Goodwood meeting. It was pretty hopeless; the performance in a straight line and on acceleration was fine but modern 1000cc Coopers gained yards on me at every corner. There was no way I could keep up with them and I saw no point in killing myself trying so I just sat back and enjoyed the ride.

It was good fun though, so I entered it for the opening Prescott. I felt it might be suitable for this event as there was plenty of power low down

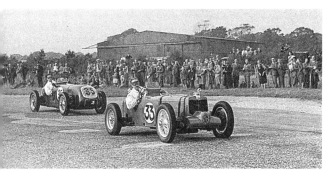 

Left: *George Dunham's Alvis (No. 35) despite its ungainly appearance was an extremely successful Brooklands car and at this point had caught me up at the end of Lavant Straight at the entry to Woodcote. In the early days there was no chicane at Goodwood and a fast entry to Woodcote was crucially important on the final lap.*

Right: *The fact that I appear to be out on my own here at Goodwood in the first meeting of September 18 could be a good or bad sign, but I was certainly enjoying myself and finished the race. In those days of course it was considered OK to wear clean overalls but a helmet at this level of racing was considered to be slightly cissy.*

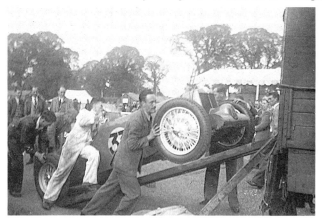

After a most enjoyable day's racing we pushed the K3 up into the faithful ex-Army Ford V8 transporter for the return to Walton. The car was all in one piece; unlike the HRG of **Motor's** *Joe Lowrey; the driver managing to up end it on the Lavant Straight which caused quite a stir at the time although nobody was hurt.*

Opposite top: *This shot is taken on my first go at Prescott, driving the still unfinished modified K3 Magnette (note scruffy paintwork and no cowl over blower.) Nevertheless we managed second in class.*

Right: *Prescott 1949 was so plagued by rain that* Motor Sport *headed its report "Prescott Regatta". The three of us with K3s made up a team; my partners being Frank Kennington and Johnny Marshall. Frank had a superb car which was unbeatable in the dry and Johnny Marshall was no slouch either. However, in the wet weather Kennington's thick spectacles misted up and I found the situation very much to my liking. This was the only occasion on which I was able to beat the flying Frank . . .*

Far right: *A fine shot of the K3 in the Great Auclum paddock, showing the lowered body line to good effect. The neck of the fuel fillers are at their original length and give a good indication of the extent to which the bodywork was dropped by a former owner. Although today such modifications would be unacceptable it did improve both the lines and visibility in my view. Did I really keep those wheels and brake drums as immaculate as that?*

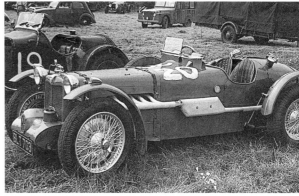

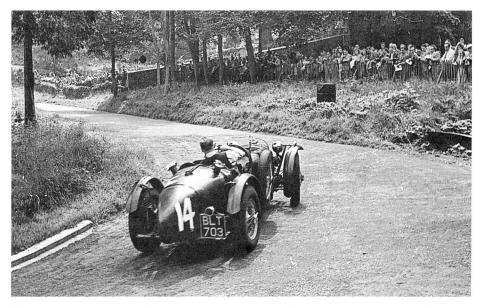

When it wasn't raining at Prescott, the setting was idyllic and here I am getting into my stride in the K3. Notice that the rules are being carefully observed; even the spare wheel in correct position for this sports car class entry.

and I had a set of twin rear wheels. I wondered about the handling but needn't have bothered as on my first practice run the blower disintegrated as I reached Pardon corner. Bits of metal flew through the bonnet and whipped around like bullets. I was thankful the blower was on the front of the engine; had it been between my legs like the later ERAs the effect on my love life could have been catastrophic! Sadly, we pushed it back into the Bedford truck I had borrowed, its total fresh air time having been about ten minutes. Fortunately, we had a box of blower parts amongst the spares acquired with the car, so during the summer I was able to make up another one.

Here is the K3 just beginning its run at Brighton in 1948. We did up our jacket buttons for the serious motoring but with a decent aero screen it wasn't necessary to worry about goggles or a visor in the dry. I have nothing but happy memories of this splendid 6-cylinder car.

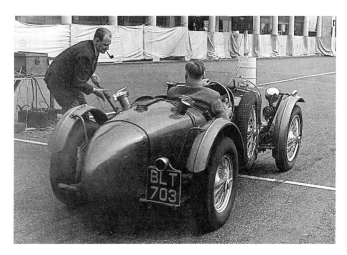

Another shot at Silverstone, with a Frazer Nash catching up on me followed by something rather stately in the rear.

The Rapier was based on a "cut and shut" chassis fitted with a very pretty narrow body which just enclosed the robust twin cam 1100cc engine. A Roots type supercharger was fitted at the front blowing a mixture of alcohol and air to produce a very useful output. Unfortunately however, by comparison with Cooper-JAPs of the same capacity, the Rapier was more than twice as heavy and had no more power to offer. Nevertheless it was a lovely car to drive.

In 1949 the offset single seater Rapier built by Roy Eccles for Brooklands Outer Circuit racing came into my hands. It was a beautiful little car and ideal for sprint races although of course no match for modern machinery on a road circuit like Goodwood where it is seen rounding St. Mary's. The famous tower in the distance is that of Graylingwell Hospital; a local landmark.

It looks as though I have a chance of catching John Cooper here, but unless one of his two plugs had gone "on the blink" I would have been outclassed. The newly harrowed infield of the circuit (the Lavant Straight can be seen in the distance) indicates that this is an early-season (Easter Monday) event.

I like this shot taken in the Goodwood paddock at that same meeting in 1949. It gives a good feel of the relaxed atmosphere of the time; still just like the Brooklands days. George, John and Bob Gerard are talking to the kneeling Cuth Harrison working on his B/C type ERA, which was a very successful car. The background is full of interest and I will leave you to work out who are the people and cars.

Meanwhile, I had a breath of the past with the British Empire Trophy and Manx Cup races on the Isle of Man at the end of May. HWM had entered three cars: the GP single seater Alta, a recently acquired Cooper 1000 – both these to be driven by Abecassis – and the 2-litre HW Alta for John Heath. The whole event, with practice sessions, took up several days and I felt I could not leave the garage for that long, so reluctantly decided not to go.

However, a few days before the races I was talking to Mike Hawthorn when he mentioned his father had two aeroplanes and was flying over for the race meeting. I knew his father, Leslie, quite well and rang him to see if he had a spare seat as a quick trip would be possible for me. He hadn't but said I could borrow the other plane if I could find a pilot. This was no problem as one of my pals had continued flying after the war, so we recruited two others to share the expenses and set off for Blackbushe. The plane was an ex-American Army Fairchild Argus, a high wing monoplane with a single radial engine. It looked a bit grotty but my friend and I both agreed we had probably flown in worse things during the war, so we took off.

The flight was uneventful except for a disconcerting rise in the oil temperature and we were soon on our way to the circuit. The first sight to greet me was Abecassis hobbling around using a pair of floor mops as crutches, having overturned the Cooper in practice. He obviously was out of the race so John Heath drove the GP car in one and the 2-litre in the other. He came nowhere in the GP but was first in the Manx Cup, a really creditable effort.

Above left: *When Charles and son John Cooper built their first post-war Specials and later went into production with 500 and 1000cc "over the counter" models, none of us could have foreseen the tremendous influence that these cars would have on the course of motor racing design. Many of the established drivers of the day were intrigued by the often phenomenal performance of these tiny cars over short distances and decided to investigate. John and George bought this 1000cc version of the car in 1949, fitted with a Vincent-HRD V-twin engine running on alcohol. The car was eligible for the current Formula B class racing (up to 2 litres u/s) and it could keep up with anything produced by Ferrari, Maserati and Co., for a couple of laps. George had a very nasty accident in the Isle of Man in this car and promptly sold it (it is now being restored in the USA); George having gone off it in a big way. Here the car is shown at Goodwood where it retired in quick order. The Vincent engine was designed to run on petrol and never really managed the transition to "dope" successfully. Still it was a much better piece of engineering than the more popular JAPs.*

Above right: *While all the fuss was going on about the V16 BRM, Geoffrey Taylor was quietly getting on with building his own Alta Grand Prix car. We had the first one produced (GP1) seen here at Goodwood in 1949. George is chewing his fingernails and wasn't having a very happy day. Alf Francis is at work on the car (bending, left).*

Needless to say this called for celebrations on the old scale and at the end of it we did not feel like flying back home so we stayed the night, the state of the two pilots being one of the reasons we made this decision! Next day I flew home with Les as he was going back by himself and wanted company. The weather was dreadful; he could not get above cloud level and at Blackbushe a howling wind was blowing across the runway. The Fairchild was a very light plane and did not take kindly to the cross wind landing Les was forced to make, but we finally bounced and swerved to a standstill and offered up a little prayer.

My prospects for further racing during 1949 looked pretty black as it was obviously going to be some time before I could rebuild the blower on the Lagonda, but once more a stroke of luck came my way.

I had received an invitation to enter a sports car race at Silverstone and a builder friend of mine suggested I use his car, another K3 Magnette. He had recently bought it as a sports car for everyday use. It was the flat tank model, more suitable for shopping than racing, but I was very grateful to

George is here accelerating past the uncovered paddock area in Alta GP1, looking rather startled and blowing a lot of smoke. The Riley 1½ litre saloon in the front is rather typical of the relaxed arrangements of the day. The Alta had a very advanced specification with all independent suspension by wishbones with rubber-in-compression springing. The 4-cylinder twin cam engine had its roots in pre-war Alta designs but it was intended to provide it with 2-stage supercharging at a later point in development. A 4-speed synchromesh gearbox of Alta construction was provided but this was the Achilles Heel of the car and frequently gave trouble. Poor Geoffrey Taylor could never really offer the sort of factory support that was available from Maserati and others and so most of the private owners gave up, us included.

At the end of the war the surplus single engined aircraft used as personal transport by high ranking officers and for general Army and Airforce liaison duties were eagerly snapped up by flying enthusiasts. Leslie Hawthorn, father of Mike, bought this Fairchild Argus, a large machine fitted with a hefty Pratt & Whitney radial (he had two of them) and he lent it me for George Leighton DFC, the chap who bought the Riley Nine, to fly to the Isle of Man TT races. If you're still around and see this George, I would love to hear from you.

him and set about making it go. With somewhat limited time I managed to get quite a bit more urge into it but could do nothing about the brakes, which were of an earlier type than those fitted to my own car and nowhere near them in efficiency.

In the event it was a silly, irritating fault that put me out of the running. The engine was fitted with a small sump and on every corner the oil surged away from the pump leaving me with no pressure. I was therefore unable to accelerate out of the corner until it had surged back again and of course this also affected the speed I went into it. I was a bit peeved about it, as to the marshals and spectators on the corners it must have looked as though I was frightened of the car. However, it was a lot of fun and I didn't finish too far down in the results.

The next event was the Great Auclum Hill Climb. I had competed there

For a Silverstone Club meeting I borrowed this standard K3, AGW 37. There was a very big difference between this car and my own pointed-tail machine but I nevertheless enjoyed the race. This car is still about and as far as I can remember belonged to a builder in "my" time.

in 1948 with my K3 but for 1949 entered an MG TC. This was a perfectly standard car but a very good one and with a little tweaking had good performance, especially low down where it was most needed.

During the summer I managed to get in a few trials and fairly local rallies but at last the Rapier's blower was rebuilt and I entered it for the Brighton Speed Trials. On the first run it went like a rocket and made best time of the pre-war racing cars in my class, but on the second run a sudden rattle caused me to switch off and I coasted to the finish with a big-end gone.

In 1949 an ex-Glider Regiment Captain came to me to learn the Garage Trade bringing with him this TC MG that he had bought from Raymond Mays at Bourne. I always thought the TC under-rated at the time but it certainly seems to have come into its own today. I borrowed the car, entered it for Great Auclum in August 1949 and was suitably impressed.

Of course the TC was in a different class in terms of both performance and roadholding from the K3, but the T Series cars were always far more practical for the amateur enthusiast. There were plenty of examples about which had been subject to the attentions of amateur and professional tuners which would have no difficulty in leaving a K3 behind in serious motor racing situations.

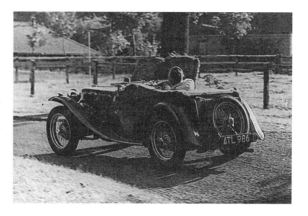

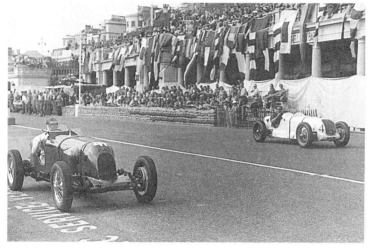

I ran the Rapier at Brighton in 1949; here against W. Bristow in a 1½ litre Alta. The Rapier put up best time for pre-war cars in this class.

This was the end of my 1949 season. To say it had been unsuccessful would be an understatement but I had enjoyed it. On the HWM front things were looking up. During the winter John had constructed the car which gave him victory in the Manx Cup. He had decided to make a car that could be used for sports car races, stripped out to compete in Formula 2 and, at the same time, was perfectly usable on the road. The chassis consisted of tubular members, transverse leaf spring IFS and quarter elliptic springs at the rear. Front suspension and stub axles were Standard 14, Citroën rack and pinion was used and the rear axle was a spare Lagonda Rapier unit that was amongst the pile of bits purchased with the ill-fated single seater.

For the power unit the engine was removed from the streamlined Alta and fitted with an ENV pre-selector gearbox. I believe the body was built by Coopers but could be wrong. Whoever built it, I'm sure John Heath had a hand in its design. Registered NPA 5 it was driven to RAF Odiham for testing and passed with flying colours. I didn't have much to with all this; naturally I was very interested in the project and helped when necessary, but my main contribution was to relieve the others of the day to day running of the garage.

We had also acquired the new GP Alta, a splendid effort on the part of

Shortly after this shot was taken of the Rapier on its second run it ran two big ends and coasted over the line. Several people have built Specials based on the Rapier (including perhaps the most famous one constructed by Daniel Richmond of Downton) but when they are boosted to produce the sort of power that the rugged little engine looks as though it could handle, unreliability frequently creeps in even on a short run like the kilometre at Brighton.

Above left: *Happy memories were revived when I opened the course at Great Auclum many years after competing there in this Facel Vega Excellence. It was a very big car for such a twisty course but stormed up in fine style – a lot faster than the TC and TD MGs of my last serious attempts!*

Above right: *I received the honour of opening the Great Auclum course no less than three times and on this occasion am doing it with a DB4. The third occasion was at the wheel of a Facel Vega KH500. It was very enjoyable to drive up well within the car's capabilities and without the pressure of competition.*

Geoffrey Taylor bearing in mind his limited resources. Unfortunately, although the car was fast and handled well, it proved extremely unreliable. Both cars were entered for the Easter Monday meeting at Goodwood. The GP gave gearbox trouble but John managed a fourth place in the HW Alta. Jersey brought no better luck, but in the British Grand Prix the Alta went well, carburettor trouble robbing it of a place. Various other meetings at home and abroad were attended but the only real success was the Manx Cup previously mentioned.

During the winter I had two tasks. Firstly the bearings on the Rapier had to be done prior to selling it, secondly there was work to do on my old K3. Friend Johnson who had bought it decided to enter the last Prescott meeting, went off the road and hit a tree. There was a fair amount of damage but it was repairable, so it was loaded on to a trailer and sent back to us. Once more it was stripped to the bare chassis frame and work commenced,

John Heath got a bee in his bonnet about making his own racing car and being a very practical man got on with it immediately. His first really new effort was the HW Alta shown here at Goodwood. The idea was that the car could be run with or without road equipment in sports car and Formula Two events. It had a 2-litre unsupercharged engine fitted with twin SU carburettors and a pre-selector gearbox. The chassis was a simple twin tube type with a conventional rear axle on quarter elliptic springs. The front suspension was based on Standard 14 components and although rather heavy and underpowered John achieved some notable successes with it at home and abroad. The car is still in use today.

Here is a shot of the HW Alta from the carburettor side showing the twin SUs fed by fuel pumps driven off the rear of the camshafts. Alta engines were nearly all different but this is a very nice one with the camshafts driven in the best fashion from the rear of the crankshaft by chain, with water and oil pumps at the front of the power unit where leaking seals would often allow the two fluids to mix and emulsify.

straightening and trueing-up the chassis and front axle being the first job. The owner then asked if we could convert it to hydraulic brakes. I was unhappy about this. In these days, of course, it would be considered sacrilege to depart from the original specification, but in 1949 nobody bothered about such things and my objections were purely technical. The chassis frame was

This is my last race in the K3; taken at Lulsgate in 1950. I managed 3rd in the scratch race but was unplaced in a handicap following an over-enthusiastic spin. I used this meeting as a sort of testing session to check the car after we had rebuilt it following a shunt by the new owner at the last Prescott meeting of 1949.

a flimsy affair; if one person stood at one end and the other was held rigid it was possible to twist the frame through about 20 degrees. I was certain it was this flexibility which gave the car such good roadholding. There was little give in the suspension on corners but the twisting chassis gave it a kind of primitive IFS. To absorb the torque of powerful hydraulic brakes it would be necessary to stiffen up the chassis frame.

However, it was his car and he was paying for it so a new crossmember was made up and welded in, the side members boxed in and fishplates welded into the corners. It was not too difficult to fit wheel cylinders into the existing back plates, find a suitable master cylinder and make up the pipes. Whilst the engine was out it was opened up, found to be perfect and put back together.

The car was ready early in 1950 and, as I had been invited to a race meeting at Lulsgate, the owner agreed to my entering it as a sort of test run. I entered for a scratch race and a handicap. The new brakes worked quite well and I was well satisfied with my third place in the face of some pretty stiff opposition. I had been given a good handicap for my next race but my 3rd place earlier changed their minds and I was put back a bit. I found myself on the line with the vintage Bentleys. I had one either side, towering above me, their drivers grinning down at me, engines throbbing as only a vintage Bentley can. Thus intimidated, I made a poor start but soon caught up as the K3 had better acceleration and was nippier on corners.

Opposite top: *Here is a good shot of George Abecassis at speed in my favourite Aston, the DB2 at Le Mans 1950, showing the car's wonderful lines to advantage.*

Opposite bottom: *George Abecassis passes the pits in the 1950 Le Mans race. The Index of Performance-winning DB2 has a distinctly Italian look about it and the Vee windscreen is very much of the period. The one-piece lifting bonnet was heavy but ideal for competition, giving access to engine and front suspension in a matter of seconds. In the background of this shot is the rather improbable 2½ litre Riley entered by Lawrie Beeston which surprisingly finished in 17th place.*

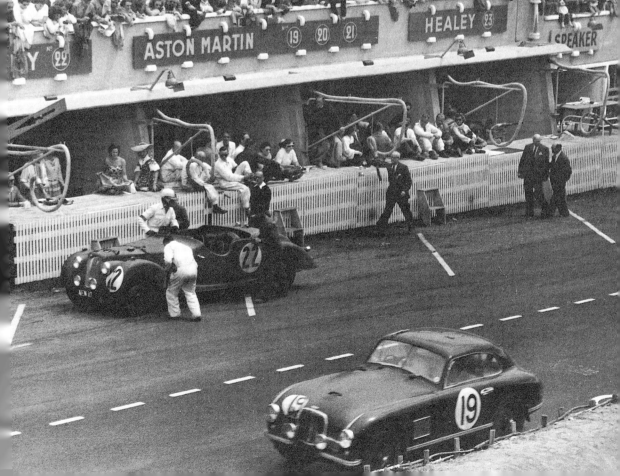

After $3\frac{1}{2}$ laps I had caught up and passed some of the earlier starters and could see a gaggle of cars in the distance. I knew these must be the first ones off and that, with a lap and a half to go, I could catch them easily. Suddenly a Bentley appeared in my mirror. Obviously he was catching me and I had to go a bit faster. Leaving my braking a bit later I went into the next corner very fast, spun round and went off the track backwards, fortunately without hitting anything. Much chastened I re-entered the race and finished seventh. Anyone who spins off has only himself to blame so I am not making any excuses when I say it probably wouldn't have happened with my old flexible chassis.

I couldn't see much prospect of racing in 1950 and more or less resigned myself to spectating and assisting. I had rebuilt the Rapier during the winter but there was no reason to suppose it would be any more reliable than previously, so as it had very little chance of success anyway it went into retirement and was eventually sold.

My pal Stephen had replaced his MG TC with a TD, a much more civilised car but heavier and not as fast. To give it a bit more steam we fitted a supercharger; this certainly improved matters and the car went very well. I entered it for Great Auclum, just for the ride, really, as I knew it had no chance of success, the blower putting it in a class far beyond its capabilities. I finished well down in the results but thoroughly enjoyed it, the little car being delightfully stable.

The arrival on the scene in 1936 of the TA MG was a huge shock for MG enthusiasts. When the TD MG came out in 1950 with a specification tailored for the vital US market, those of us who had by then adjusted to the TC were equally shaken. However, although the TD is a very different animal from its immediate predecessor it was extremely practical for the private owner; although not particularly fast in standard form. This shot is taken at Great Auclum and shows me waiting in Stephen's TD fitted with a low-pressure blower which gave the car a little more poke. Sadly it meant that it had to enter in the 2-litre class in which it was unable to make much impact.

We then decided to enter it for a Goodwood meeting as Stephen wished to try his luck. We were down for two races, a scratch race for Stephen and a handicap for me. The magic word 'supercharged' was enough to get me a ridiculous handicap, so once more I was just in it for the ride. As it happened I didn't even get that apart from practice. Stephen's race came first and about halfway through the oil pipe to the blower fractured, pumping oil out and making a shocking mess. By the time we got the car back to the pits, repaired the pipe and cleaned everything up my race had started.

We did a few trials and minor rallies in it during the year, the best one

Here is the TD shortly after the start at Great Auclum. It was certainly faster than my previous year's effort in the TC. The TD could not really by compared with the TC; it was altogether a "softer" car; a transition between pre-war and post-war British sports car thinking.

being the MG Car Club's Chiltern Trial, but didn't aspire to race it again. Activity continued in the racing department of the garage. The success of NPA 5 prompted John Heath to embark on an ambitious scheme to build a team of three cars and a prototype. It was a terrific undertaking for such a small company but he was determined to do it and he did.

The cars were based on the HW Alta, the main difference being transverse leaf spring IRS. The 2-litre Alta engine was retained, somewhat modified and Armstrong Siddeley gearboxes used instead of ENV. I seem to remember this was due to supply problems with ENV rather than technical superiority but as it happened the Armstrong boxes proved completely reliable. A rather poor showing at the Goodwood Easter Monday meeting did not deter anybody. We had a team of three cars and a spare and they performed well, they looked good and their immaculate turn out impressed everyone. Once more my main contribution to the project was looking after the shop and this was even more important when the team embarked on an extensive continental tour at the end of April. The tour itself was a mixture of success and failure as far as results were concerned but from the point of view of British prestige it was an overwhelming success. More than anything it put Great Britain on the motor racing map and we were all very proud of them.

The following year I managed to get one race in. I made a poor showing and would prefer to forget it but to make my story complete it should be recorded. One of our customers was a senior RAF officer, Air Commodore Worsley. He was very motor racing-conscious, his wife being a pre-war racing

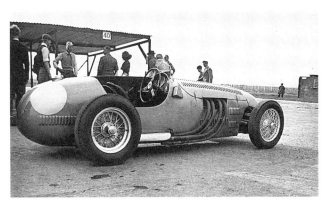

Having been so pleased with the results of the first attempt at building a "proper" racing car John set about producing a more up-to-date version which became the first HWM. Here is the prototype on test at Goodwood (George in the background). The new car had independent rear as well as front suspension and 4 separate long exhaust pipes, making a lot of noise and stench immediately below the driver's nose. Although, as in the case of the HW-Alta, the original intention was to run these cars in both sports car and racing events they were too busily engaged in Formula Two racing to have time for the alternative. Eventually a team of three cars was completed and campaigned with considerable success.

One of our most successful drivers of the first HWMs was the young Stirling Moss, here showing off his curly hair to advantage. The photograph was taken in March 1950 on a cold practice day for the Easter Monday races at Goodwood. The car's primitive independent suspension by lightly modified Standard 14 components is shown clearly and this feature of the car gave us a lot of trouble. If you want to know more about the HWM racing saga read Alf Francis' splendid book.

driver of great repute. He purchased a very stark Alvis Speed 20 and wanted to race it in the Eight Clubs Meeting at Silverstone. As I belonged to one of the Eight Clubs he asked me to enter it, naming him as the driver in the One Hour Blind and myself in a scratch race. He drove impeccably and put up a jolly good performance.

My race was the last on the programme and I wasn't happy at all. For a start I couldn't get a comfortable driving position as he was much taller than me and obviously the car was set up for him. Then I normally drove bareheaded but we had a customer who made miners' helmets. He wanted to get into the crash helmet business and asked me to wear a prototype. I didn't get a chance to practice in it but put it on for the race. It was a

Here I am (wearing a crash helmet at last) in the last race of my career, at Silverstone and driving the Speed Twenty Alvis owned by Air Commodore Worsley. If he is still around and reads this I would like to know if he ever received his award at the same meeting. My performance can only be described as dreadful, even though we had gone to the length of rotating the headlamps through 90 degrees to reduce drag . . .

dreadful thing; the chin strap had a certain amount of elasticity and the helmet kept lifting. I couldn't remote it altogether as my goggles were attached to it and it was very distracting. To make everything even more off-putting the engine and transmission were very noisy. My own Air Force days were not that far behind and the thought to blowing up an Air Commodore's pride and joy was a bit daunting.

To complete the aggro the gallant officer should have received a plaque or something for his performance in the One Hour Blind. As the entrant it would have come to me but naturally I would have given it to him. I never received it in spite of contacting both the organisers and my own Club. I am certain he thought I had kept it but was too much of a gentleman to say so, and I felt most awkward.

On the HWM front a team of single seater Formula 2 cars had been constructed during the winter, still using Alta engines and a tubular frame but with coil spring front suspension (from memory I think it was MG TD), Morris Minor steering rack instead of Citroën and a de Dion rear end. The original team cars were sold. One went to Switzerland, bought by Fergus Anderson, a racing motorcyclist who had driven the odd race for us. He was not a Swiss but as he raced bikes extensively on the continent I suppose he found it convenient to live there. Oscar Moore purchased one and two amateur drivers bought the others.

One of these was Tom Meyer, a wealthy timber merchant who had previously bought the streamlined Alta. I remember that when he bought the second one Tom O'Hara, one of the racing mechanics, went with him to look after it. Ton Meyer also owned as magnificent open $4\frac{1}{2}$-litre Bentley that had been in his family since new. Over 30 years later I was at the Bentley Drivers' Club meeting in Kensington Gardens and there he was. He still had the Bentley and still had Tom O'Hara to maintain it. He was there as

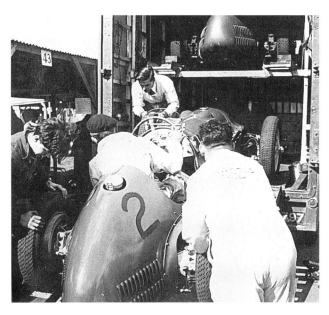

Here is a good shot of two of the 1950 monoposto HWM cars being unloaded at Goodwood. Alf Francis is at the wheel and the late Frank Nagle is supervising the nearside front wheel. These cars had stub exhausts which were fashionable at the time and front suspension based on MG components, which were more reliable than the earlier Standard-derived type. The massive de Dion tube and lever-type rear dampers can be clearly seen. These cars, like the earlier HWMs made excellent Specials when fitted with gutsy Jaguar engines.

well and we all had a good natter about old times.

The HWM single seaters went on another ambitious continental tour. Stirling Moss, George Abecassis and Lance Macklin were the main drivers but several others had a go, including Bira. The cars achieved several second and third places although no outright wins, but lots of problems had been solved, much experience gained and once more a British team, immaculately turned out, had shown the flag. It is my opinion that John Heath did not receive anywhere near the credit he deserved for his efforts during this and subsequent years. It is true that with the present day interest in bygone years his contribution to motor racing is being recognised, but a little more encouragement when he was still alive would have meant a lot to him. A think he did a marvellous job and I'm proud to have been associated with him and the project, even though relatively speaking I was not very much involved.

My own efforts from then on were confined to trials, the odd one day rally and driving tests. I was quite happy about this; I had no illusions about my own capabilities and knew I would never be another Stirling Moss. On the other hand what racing I had done over the preceding four years had given me tremendous pleasure, I hadn't disgraced myself and I hadn't got hurt. Moreover, the experience I gained undoubtedly helped when later on testing and demonstrating high speed cars became part of my job.

The HWMs were modified for 1952 in an attempt to obtain more speed and reliability. Another continental tour was organised and once more a team of green cars competed with Europe's best. Stirling had left the team but Lance Macklin was still with us, being joined by Peter Collins. Once more John Heath had picked a winner as he had with Stirling and both were to become household names in future years. They had previously done well in Formula 3 but it was John who gave them their chance to prove they could handle something bigger and faster. Several well known drivers,

My pal Stephen lent his Aston Martin DB2 to Abecassis for a race at Snetterton in 1952. It went extraordinarily well driven by the capable George but Stephen swore that it was never the same car again. Everything felt very loose.

including Tony Rolt, Duncan Hamilton and Giraud-Cabantous drove HWMs during the year, a sure sign that the cars had become accepted as serious competition in Formula 2.

The following year the pre-selector gearbox was abandoned in favour of a normal manual box. I probably knew the reason for the change at the time but cannot recall it now. I do remember the clutch gave a certain amount of trouble and once more an outright victory evaded the team. Sometime previously Oscar Moore had fitted his early HWM with a Jaguar engine. Its performance was not lost on John Heath and, with the demise of Formula 2 in 1954, he decided to do the same and concentrate on sports car races. I remember new Jaguar engines were unobtainable so he would tour the breakers' yards looking for smashed MkVIIs, buying the engines and gearboxes. Various modifications were made to them including fitting three twin choke Webers. These sports cars became just as well known as the single seaters and are collectors' items today. They were fantastic cars to drive on the road and one I particularly liked was the hill climb car built for Phillip

As the HWM Formula 2 cars became obsolete, one or two of them were converted into interesting high-class Specials. This rear view however shows the Alta-Jaguar built for Phillip Scragg on the GP Alta chassis for hill climbing; a combination which was unbeatable for a very long time. I took this picture when out on test in the early stages of the car's life.

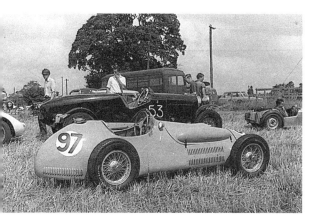

Above left: *Here is another HWM given a new lease of life with a Jaguar engine. This is the version raced for many years by Rivers Fletcher and based on our single seater of 1950/51. This was a car which was quite capable of handling a lot more power than given by the standard 2 litre Alta engine and the Jaguar suited it very well.*

Above right: *The Tourist Trophy races have moved around in their time but here is a photograph taken in their heyday at Goodwood showing Stirling Moss catching up an Aston Martin at the chicane. Stirling is driving the Rob Walker short wheel base Ferrari 250 GT with which he was virtually unbeatable in this type of racing. The Walker car was one of the few with right-hand drive and must have been difficult to drive although SM made it look the easiest thing in the world, as usual.*

Scragg. The GP Alta chassis was used for this car.

I did some of the initial testing and loved it, preferring the stark body and close fitting wings to the all enveloping design of the other cars. It went like the proverbial rocket; Phillip was virtually unbeatable and made FTD so many times the opposition must have become resigned to it. He was one of the nicest chaps in the game and his death was a terrible shock.

For the next two years the sports cars were raced extensively. Most of the top line drivers had a go in them at one time or another and a reasonable amount of success was achieved. The cars acquitted themselves well in the face of stiff competition from factory teams, all with vast resources compared with HWM.

With all this going on it was a terrible tragedy then John Heath died as a result of injuries received in the 1956 Mille Miglia. There were various peculiar things about his accident. Firstly, he didn't want to go and had none of his usual enthusiasm for it. When a hitch arose – something to do with his RAC permit or his insurance you could see he was relieved although naturally he made out he was disappointed. Then, at the last minute, the problem was resolved so he had no option but to set off. The race was run in pouring rain and he had covered a relatively short distance when, on a notoriously slippery section, he was blinded by spray from an overtaking car and went off the road. The HWM-Jaguar car itself suffered an incredibly small amount of damage. Nobody mixed up in racing for years could fail to have seen many shunts. In a lot of them the cars have been virtual write-offs but the drivers have walked away unhurt, yet here we had poor John Heath, with very little more damage than a bashed-in door, receiving fatal injuries.

His death cast a shadow over the garage for a long time. The racing and construction programme came to a halt and the existing cars were sold. There was a partly-built chassis and enough parts to complete it and this was completed as a sports coupé. It was a beautiful job, sleek, stylish, with every comfort available at that time and not many purely road going coupé could match its performance. I often wonder if it still exists. The end of the HWMs marked the end of my involvement in motor racing except as a spectator. Very soon the whole character of it was to change anyway. Present day GP cars do nothing for me at all and sports cars will always be cars that can be driven sensibly on the roads as well as the track as far as I am concerned. Fortunately, Historic and Vintage Car racing has become popular in recent years and the Clubs concerned do a marvellous job. I attend these meetings whenever I can and at the last one I even smelt some Castrol R. Surely there can be nothing more nostalgic than that!

6
SIX YEARS OF FACEL VEGA

For a variety of reasons, mostly economic, the post-war years have been sadly lacking in large, powerful and exotic motor cars of the type usually associated with the continent. Moreover, a generation of motorists has come into being to whom names like Hispano-Suiza, Isotta Fraschini, Delage, etc., are in fact just names, the cars themselves being completely outside their range of experience.

It was not surprising, therefore, that the advent of the Facel Vega caused a considerable stir and a fair amount of controversy. There were two schools of thought. Firstly, the people who appreciated the incredible performance coupled with the silence of an American power unit and, secondly, people who like to see a nicely turned out unit, polished camshaft covers and the like. Everybody was in agreement over the roadholding, handling, performance, the luxurious interior and the distinctive lines. I must admit to liking a nice looking engine bay myself.

As I was closely associated with the Facel since the first car was imported in 1957, I still receive enquiries concerning the car and its background, and hope the following brief history of the car in the UK together with some

Rather out of context but very important in the Facel Vega story. This picture shows Jean Daninos, President and Patron of the company during the production, shown with a Facel 2. The occasion was the 1986 Paris to Deauville Rally.

personal experiences will be of interest.

As the origin of the car is rather obscure a few notes on this subject are appropriate. Facel SA was created in 1939. In fact M. Daninos, the joint President, initiated the basic productions of the company in 1938. These were later on reflected in their industrial specialities as well as in their manufacturing side.

At the beginning of its operations Facel specialised in the production of large tools and dies for the aircraft and automobile industries.

In late 1939 a second plant was opened for the manufacture and assembly of aircraft products and at the beginning of the war more than 50 per cent of their production was devoted to the French defence effort. When the war ended in France during 1940, one of the Facel factories was occupied by the Germans and the other manufactured wood burning condensors for the operation of trucks and lorries.

After the war the company was reorganised and in 1946 commenced making car bodies for various French manufacturers. Production of complete cars started in 1955 with the FVS model.

The car was evolved to get the best of both worlds by using a French chassis and body with an American engine. It had been done successfully before in England with the Railton, Allard, etc., but previously the French had relied on their own power units. The engine in the FVS was a Chrysler V8 of 4,940 cc, developing 260 bhp at 4,600 rpm, with the usual push rod ohv, hydraulic tappets and single downdraught four choke carburettor mounted in the centre of the vee. The chassis was of tubular steel, coil spring IFS and semi-elliptic leaf springs at the rear, locating a normal Salisbury hypoid axle. Damping was by telescopic shock absorbers. In other words, a perfectly ordinary, rather 'old fashioned' chassis which in fact continued to the end of production with very little alteration. Transmission initially was by Chrysler two-speed automatic gearbox driven via a torque converter. This was later changed to a three-speed unit and in 1957 a four-speed all synchromesh gearbox, manufactured by Pont à Mousson was offered as an option. Two carburettors were fitted to this model.

Brakes were hydraulic, servo-assisted, with two leading shoes on the front and large, heavily-ribbed composite aluminium drums. All cars were, naturally, left hand drive.

The coachwork was a two door coupé, a comfortable two seater with two seats at the rear for children or emergency use. The first cars had a normal windscreen with stainless steel pillars but this was later changed to a full wrap around. The standard of finish was high, the upholstery was in English Conolly hide and equipment included heater, radio with automatic electrically-operated aerial and electric windows. The last two items are common now but were unusual thirty years ago.

The Facel Vega, as it was now called, was only available on the continent until 1957 when one was imported to England for Mr. Arnold Burton, of tailoring fame, through, I believe, Boltons of Leeds. Some time previous to this Lance Macklin, who resided in Paris, had joined the company on the export sales side and came over to England to find an English concessionaire. It was natural that he first approached HW Motors, for he had been one of our team drivers in the days of the HWM, knew George Abecassis personally and also knew of our tendency to go in for exciting motor cars. Furthermore we had the staff and facilities for servicing. As a result we imported our first car in May 1957 and proceeded to sort out its possibilities in the United Kingdom, firstly as regards the car itself and secondly as a commercial proposition. This car was fitted with the synchromesh gearbox and, being finished in silver with red interior, caused quite a sensation.

We ran the car ourselves, Abecassis using it as personal transport, and reached several conclusions. Firstly, we considered more power was necessary if the car was to make an impact on the high performance luxury market. We therefore purchased a 6-litre Chrysler V8 engine which gave 325 bhp at 4,500 rpm.

It differed considerably from the original and many modifications were necessary, but when finally fitted it transformed the car. It now really motored. This unfortunately accentuated the second fault – the brakes were hopelessly inadequate for very high speeds. Not only did we have unpleasant moments whilst trying to stop the car from speeds over a hundred miles per hour, but the heat generated in the drums was such that they lasted no time at all. It was obvious discs were going to be needed.

These things apart the car was a proposition, the interest in it was tremendous and we decided to take up the concession, subject to (i) right hand drive being available. (ii) A more powerful engine being fitted. (iii) Disc brakes. (iv) Various minor alterations being made to suit the English market. In the meantime we had sold and delivered one car to the original specification to a well known Baronet, which was rather encouraging.

In July 1958 the first batch of rhd cars came over. It was now a much nicer car and designated the HK500. The engine was still a Chrysler V8 but

Here is a snapshot of an HK500 taken on the playing fields of Sandhurst Military College.

of 5,907 cc and developing 360 bhp at 4,800 rpm with two four-barrel downdraught carburettors operating on a graduated throttle. Developed especially for Facel it was named the 'Typhoon'. Disc brakes were not available for the first nine cars and the first three had bolt-on wire wheels instead of the later centre-lock type. In due course, as parts became available, we converted all these cars to Dunlop disc brakes with centre-lock wheels

My own HK500 photographed in my front drive. This car was originally sold to the Marchioness of Huntley via the agency of Charles Follett. A beautiful car.

to the first three.

The first batch sold at once but, as before, we kept one for demonstrations, Abecassis' personal use and to use as a 'guinea pig'. This car did 25,000 miles in our hands and was exemplary. We carried out numerous experiments with such things as plugs, brake pads, dampers, etc., and the car, when sold, carried on to a mileage of 52,000 when I last saw it in November 1962. Its present whereabouts is unknown.

By October we had sold ten cars, had a stand at the Motor Show and felt we had 'arrived'. A lot of interest was created at the Show and we were able to order another batch of cars. By that time the business was beginning to overload HWM and in due course a new company was formed to handle the franchise. It was registered as InterContinental Cars Ltd, with George Abecassis as Managing Director, the same position he held with HWM, myself as Service or Technical Director, also as per HWM, and Tim Greenley as Sales Director.

Here is a shot of the Facel Excellence taken in a rural setting. The Excellence was certainly an impressive carriage but spoilt by many shortcomings in the construction of the body. Its huge weight resulted in a lot of trouble with the heavily overloaded drum brakes which were only converted to discs at a much later stage in the car's development.

Many more cars were sold and in April 1959 we had the first two HK500s with automatic gearbox and power steering. These were fitted with a single carburettor engine developing 330 bhp at 4,500 rpm and a back axle ratio of 3.31 to 1 instead of the normal 2.93. Acceleration was about the same but top speed dropped from 130 mph to 120.

At this time we also had our first Excellence. This model had been produced in France since early 1958 and was awaited with interest. With an overall length of seventeen feet three inches, a four door pillarless body, the then fashionable tail fins, etc., it was an imposing vehicle and handled much better than one would expect. The engine was the 330 bhp unit, axle ratio 3.31 to 1 and power steering was standard.

Unfortunately with the particular form of bolt on disc wheels fitted it had to be content with drum brakes and these were a constant source of trouble on all Excellence models until discs were fitted in late 1960. The pillarless construction was not really a success either and the doors were constantly in need of attention.

July 1959 saw the introduction of the 1960 model. Rather early, it is true, but the continentals are apt to do this. Apart from minor improvements, the engine size was increased to 6,286 cc, developed 390 bhp at 5,400 rpm for the two carburetter synchromesh car and 355 bhp at 4,800 rpm for the automatic. Another modification was the introduction of perforated steel disc wheels instead of wire spokes. Centre lock fitting was still used. These wheels were, in fact, a major disaster on the first batch of cars, as they began to split around the centre where the wheel was riveted to the hub. This was accompanied by the shearing of the rivet heads. This was not at all funny on a 130 mph car weighing nearly two tons, and my priority task was to do something about it smartly!

I contacted a local engineering concern specialising in forms of riveting, electro-welding, etc., and we experimented with a set of wheels. We could not be certain whether the rivet heads were breaking off and causing the wheel to split or whether the wheels were splitting first. We finally decided it was the latter and modified the wheels accordingly. Meanwhile the wheel manufacturers had been called in by Facel and pinpointed the source of the trouble as starting from holes drilled near the hub to locate a centre embellisher.

Modified wheels were quickly brought out and I hurried over to Paris in a large estate car, returning with thirty new wheels which were promptly dispatched to the six owners concerned. No further trouble was experienced.

Another trouble arose from the fitting of a more powerful engine as we shortly began experiencing failure of third gear. It was pretty obvious that the extra power was just too much for it and after a few failures I went over to Pont-à-Mousson at Sens and discussed the matter with their gearbox specialist, Mr Pugh, who turned out to be an Englishman. In spite of our discussion and the willingness of Mr Pugh, none of our suggestions were adopted and we still broke third gears. Eventually (probably because of the number of guarantee claims we sent in!) they modified the gears, but for some reason or other refused to radius the bottom of the teeth as I suggested. These new gears were better but still broke too frequently to be acceptable and finally they modified them again with a radius as I had originally requested. These later gears gave very little trouble and it is typical of the French that so much effort and unnecessary expense should be required before results were obtained. When the 1959 Show came round we were well established and had sold thirty-three cars. They had acquired a certain amount of prestige value and many notable people had purchased them.

We treated ourselves to a new demonstrator, 10 LPJ, and this was kept busy for a long time as a result of Show enquiries. The demonstrations were carried out either by George Abecassis or myself and took place all over the country. Trips to Liverpool, Grimsby, Cornwall, etc., were quite usual and as most people interested in the car wanted a long demonstration run, the day's mileage could easily be anything from five to seven hundred.

As it was winter time conditions were not always too good and it speaks well for the car that I was very seldom tired at the end of the trip. Life was made easier later on as stretches of motorway were opened, but initially all the driving had to be done on normal roads.

1960 saw no changes in specification and the highlight of the year was probably a timed run of 150 mph by Maurice Trintingnant on a continental motorway. Disc brakes also became standard on the Excellence in early September.

During the year the company had been producing a four cylinder small Facel in France which was announced at the 1959 Paris Salon and we obtained the first rhd versions in September 1960, just in time for the Show. It was designated the Facellia.

This car was eagerly awaited; the chassis was a scaled down version of the HK500, but the engine was of their own design made in conjunction with Pont-à-Mousson.

The specification looked promising: twin overhead camshafts carried in ball bearings, detachable wet cylinder liners, a five bearing crankshaft, twin choke downdraught carburetter, a capacity of 1,647 cc, a compression ratio of 9.4 to 1 and a claimed 115 bhp at 6,400 rpm. Unfortunately the

Our first Facellia with Hilda and the inevitable dog. We used this car as a demonstrator and for trying out various modifications. At one stage I drove it back to Paris for further work to be carried out.

performance was disappointing. Although the claimed top speed of 112 mph was there the power low down was poor, the engine only really starting to get going over 3,500 rpm. Moreover, reliability was not as good as it should have been, quite serious problems being experienced. Handling, steering and braking were first class and after we had insisted on better seats and a higher standard of interior finish, it was a nice car to drive. It created a lot of interest at the Show but the price was high and sales were disappointing.

To give Facel their due, they tried hard to improve the engine. They designed a new cylinder head to improve the breathing and made various other changes but with very limited success. Eventually they fitted the P1800 Volvo engine and gearbox in it, transforming it into an extremely nice little car. It could only be made in lhd which killed it for the UK market, but I drove them a lot in France and sold one to a lady in Guernsey where I had spent holidays and got to know a few people. I collected this car from Paris, drove to Cherbourg where Silver City were operating an air ferry to the Channel Isles, and flew it across. A very enjoyable trip.

The HK500 continued unaltered until the Paris Salon of 1961 when it was replaced by the Facel II. This was basically the same chassis except for the power steering and this unit was completely redesigned. Instead of the pump operating a separate hydraulic ram connected to the track rod it now operated directly in the steering box. The whole assembly was designed and built by Hydrosteer of Luton and was a vast improvement. All Facel IIs had it as standard, whether automatic or manual.

A publicity photo of the Facel 2 put out by the factory in late 1961 when the car was announced. My first drive in this model was in a factory demonstrator that we borrowed for Earls Court. I had to bring it back from the Show in the middle of the rush hour. It was dark, pouring with rain, the car was left-hand drive, very wide indeed, and the headlamps set up for continental driving. I was threatened with all sorts of dreadful consequences if I scratched it, as a result of which I found it a very miserable ride.

The coachwork for the Facel 2 was completely redesigned. Gone was the wrap-around windscreen with its 'dog leg', which some people objected to. The rear window was larger and the whole car was lower, neater and more sleek in appearance. Moving the fuel tank to an underslung position allowed

This is a very rare car, the Facel 6. Fitted with the 3-litre 6-cylinder Austin engine it was a nice, smooth car to drive and very lively. Only a few were made and none was right-hand drive; none having been exported to the UK. This photograph was taken in France.

a much larger boot.

The cars with automatic transmission had a beautiful centre stick for gear selection, a big improvement on the previous push buttons on the dashboard. Performance was about the same as the HK500 except for the last few cars which were fitted with a 6,765 cc engine.

The Facel 6 was also being produced in Paris but only a few were built. For some time Daninos had wanted to put a British engine of around $2\frac{1}{2}$/3-litres in a slightly lengthened Facellia. At one stage we purchased a Daimler 2.5 V8 in the hope that this could be used. The various technical problems could have been overcome but the engine was expensive and the whole operation would have cost so much the car would not have been a commercial proposition. Pity really, as it would have preceded the MGB V8 by a good few years.

The 3-litre 6-cylinder BMC engine was finally chosen in the form used in the Austin Healey 3000. It was a bit too heavy but beefing up the front suspension more or less overcame that and the car handled quite well. It was very flexible, with plenty of poke low down. I used the factory cars sometimes when over there and found it a good car in Paris, where good acceleration and brakes are essential to one's survival.

None were imported over here but I saw one advertised secondhand a few years back so presume someone brought one over privately. Needless to say I wish now I had bought it.

I collected most of the new cars myself and made regular visits there to collect spares, sometimes taking a new car back for modification or to be rectified.

I found it difficult to understand the French outlook at times. How they could be so sensible and logical about some things and highly illogical in others remained a mystery to me even after six years of dealing with them.

Soon after the Facellia was first imported I took one to Paris for them to check the engine for certain modifications. Arriving at the Service Dept. around mid morning, two chaps pounced on the car with commendable speed and efficiency dismantled the engine to the extent required, reassembling with equal speed after checking. Around five o'clock the job was finished and I was just congratulating myself on being able to leave Paris before the rush hour when disaster stuck. Sheepishly they informed me they had no oil to refill the sump. This seemed so incredible, even for them, that I just

One of our first Facel 2 taken at Englefield Green in Surrey en route for delivery to Scotland. This car was finished in Bright Red with chrome wire wheels and looked a real picture, as well as going like a rocket.

couldn't believe it, but it was so and after a little conference a mechanic set off with a gallon can and some francs to buy some.

About three quarters of an hour went by and he had not returned. I knew there was a BP station about 10 minutes down the road and was getting a bit steamed up, when one of the executives walked in. He spoke English so I was able to tell him the score. He tackled the foreman and a frightful argument ensued from which I was able to gather that they did in fact have some oil, but it was Shell.

On hearing this I was pretty fed up and asked why they hadn't put it in. Excitedly he pointed to the plate under the bonnet which said use 'Mobiloil'. They had no 'Mobiloil', so that was that, no oil! I pleaded with them to put in anything. I wouldn't mind, tell no-one, would drain it out as soon as I got home if they liked, but I had to get to Le Touquet that evening ready for the first plane in the morning. After a long discussion someone had a bright idea. If they poured in the Shell from a 'Mobiloil' can that would not be so bad, so they solemnly did that and work resumed.

The amusing sequel was when, after the job was complete, tested, etc., I shook hands all round, was wished 'Bon Voyage' and was just about to start off when up panted the unfortunate wretch who had gone for the oil. He had been out two hours and was literally on his knees, having presumably walked all over Paris looking for 'Mobiloil'. Triumphantly he held up the tin. His rage when casually told it was no longer required, and the scene which followed was like something out of a French comedy and completely restored my good humour.

In the early stage of the Facel 2 we suddenly experienced a spate of automatic gearbox failures, six cars being involved. All cars had the same symptoms. Three were returned to us and the other three were stranded in various parts of the country. I got on to Paris who said, in effect, that their cars were alright, it must be the way we drove them and anyway they had no spare parts. I didn't believe this for a moment so rang up Chrysler in Antwerp, who handled their entire operation throughout Europe. They freely admitted that a batch of gearboxes had got through with faulty thrust washers, causing the main shaft to move back and grind into the back of the casing. Asked if Facel had experienced the same trouble, they said they had and 12 kits of parts were being despatched to them that afternoon and would arrive at Puteaux in the morning.

I knew that if I got back to Facel they would deny it and I would never see any of the kits, so there was only one thing to do. I had a more or less permanent 'Green Card', was Silver City's best customer, so never had any trouble in making a quick trip. I put a roof rack on my trusty Jaguar 3.4 (no, I didn't use a Facel all the time), was down at Lydd by 6.30 the next morning and caught the first flight. I arrived in Paris soon after 10, much to their astonishment.

When I told them what I had come for there were blank looks all round and, "But we told you yesterday on the phone we had no parts". I pointed to a crate by the door marked 'Chrysler' and said: "There are 12 kits in there and I want 6 of them". They protested that the box contained engine parts but I insisted it be opened. They finally conceded defeat, opened the crate and gave me the 6 kits, quite puzzled as to how I knew. The paper work was rushed through and by 11 o'clock I was on my way home, arriving back in Walton late afternoon. The three cars we had were soon being assembled and the other three kits despatched to where the other cars were situated.

You would never have thought we were on the same side. Nevertheless, they were a friendly lot and enjoyed our frequent battles of wits as much as I did.

In the meantime I had sold another Volvo-engined Facel 3. It was the one on the Show stand and was bought by a Cypriot who wanted it shipped to Switzerland, where his daughter would use it prior to it going to Cyprus. He also wanted a hard top fitted.

As the car was only in England on temporary papers, which did not include a hard top anyway, it had to go back to Paris. Customs regulations forbade its use here except for the journey from the port of entry to the Show and back again. I therefore had to collect it from Earls Court, take it straight to Lydd and thence to Paris. I then went to their Customs to get a fresh set of papers, and if you think our lot are awkward you want to try that some time. I had been through it all before when Lionel Bart insisted on having the LHD Facel 2 off the Show stand in 1961, so I knew the form, but it didn't make it any easier.

Returning to England it went into Customs bond, pending shipping documents. I later collected it and drove to Southend Airport for flying to

Switzerland.

Generally speaking the cars themselves were successful. One hundred and fifty-six were sold in the UK and they mostly gave good service. Of course there were exceptions. A certain Peer of the Realm had a real pig. Everything that could go wrong did so. One day our driver collected it from his London house; the butler came to the door with the keys and our man asked him if he knew what had to be done to it. "I will ask his Lordship" said the flunkey. Minutes later he returned and, with a perfectly straight face said, "His Lordship says, burn it". Obviously another satisfied customer!

We were conscious of the fact that people paying around £5,000 for a car expected good service and to this end kept a good stock of spare parts. We soon found the best way of making sure we got what we ordered and in reasonable time was for me to make regular trips to Paris. I would go armed with a list of requirements and while I was there would rummage through their stores, picking up a few items to add to the list. I was surprised they let me do this as I was always finding things they had previously told me were unobtainable. It may seem an expensive way of getting parts but it wasn't really. Had they been sent by rail and boat there would have been considerable freight charges, they might have hung around for days waiting Customs clearance and there would have been agents' fees to pay. Also the possibility of the crafty French sending us stuff they wanted to get rid of could not be ignored.

I used a variety of cars for this job, depending on the parts required. For body parts I took the works Morris Oxford Traveller, a surprisingly roomy vehicle. When Charlie Drake rolled his Facel 2 even this wasn't big enough! If possible I used my Jaguar 3.4 and later on did many trips in our Morris 1000 Traveller, in many ways ideal for the job and getting around Paris.

Front view of an Excellence; a very impressive looking car whatever its considerable faults may have been!

Sometimes I just took any car that was available. I remember once we were desperate for HK500 windscreens. Later on we had them made over here, but at that time hadn't found anyone to do it. They cost us £140 each, a lot of money then, and I wanted ten. The thought of £1,400 in windscreens bouncing about in the back of the Morris Oxford Traveller filled me with dismay. I measured the back seat of all the cars we had and found they would go into a Mercedes 220. It wasn't taxed so I put trade plates on for the journey to Lydd and back; once in France nobody cared if it was taxed or not. Even in this I flinched at every bump and there are plenty on French roads.

It is normal to regard Customs and Excise officers as our sworn enemies, eagerly looking for a chance to clap us in gaol, so I must say here that in roughly six years of monthly, and sometimes twice-monthly, trips for parts plus bringing in new cars, I never received anything but fair treatment and courtesy. It was not easy for them. I would often arrive at the end of the day with a car load of bits many of which would be unfamiliar to the officers concerned. The invoice was in French which they possibly could not read and they had to take me on trust to a large extent. I was careful to play fair with them and we got on fine. The only little fiddle I permitted myself was when asking about my personal loot. They would say, "Any wine?" I would reply, "Two bottles". This satisfied them and I had in fact told them the truth, but forgot to mention they were five litre bottles.

Although we did all our own mechanical work, our body repairs were sub-contracted out. We had for many years used Fulfords of Kingston who did a first class job and I believe still do. Somehow or other I had got friendly with Joe Knott, the Works Manager of a London coachbuilder, and he persuaded me to give them a few Facels. They also did a good job but were not terribly well organised. They once had an HK500 of ours for rear end damage and telephoned me in due course to say it was finished, so our driver took me up to collect it. I had a good look round, saw they had done a good job and sent my driver back home. We had a little chat, I said "cheerio", started the engine and made for the door. Within a few yards the engine stopped. Looking at the petrol gauge I saw it read empty. I knew it shouldn't be so my first thought was that someone had milked it. On the HK500 the tank is in the boot so I looked inside and found the tank was missing. Not only had they forgotten to put it back but it couldn't be found and Joe had to run me back to Walton which didn't please him much, but it was his own fault.

Although this and other odd dramas were irritating they were not serious but the last one was catastrophic for them, ourselves and the owner of the car. We had an Excellence completely burnt out, and sent it up on a trailer. It was stripped to the bare shell, cleaned, painted, the seats recovered, a new headlining put in and made ready for reassembly. It was then they discovered all the parts taken off had been thrown away with the scrap. It couldn't have happened to a worse car. The Excellence had been out of production for some time, not many were made in the first place and, although mechanical parts were not too difficult, it was impossible to obtain the innumerable parts that go into a car's interior.

I managed to supply them with instruments and a few odd bits but everything else had to be made up or fittings from other cars adapted. It took them months and must have cost them a fortune. When finished the car was a mess but it was the best they could do.

It was the last job I gave them but I stayed friendly with Joe and when later on he went to Wood and Pickett I gave him some more work. We had four demonstration cars during the Facel period, one FVS, two HK500 and one Facel 2. We also had an Excellence taken in part exchange for a short period, but sold it when the opportunity arose. All the cars did considerable mileages and led a hard life. They were all borrowed by the motoring press who usually gave them a good belting on the Continent. We had no serious trouble with any of them.

The owners represented a good cross section of the wealthy members of the community. Titled people, business tycoons, film and stage folk, racing drivers and others who would probably not admit to being wealthy but who couldn't have been that hard up. In general they were extremely pleasant people to deal with. Obviously we had the odd one or two we could have done without but it didn't take long to weigh them up and act accordingly.

There were plenty of amusing incidents. One character asked us to calibrate his speedometer 20 mph slow as his wife would not let him drive at more than a hundred. Another one didn't realise his fascia panel was metal painted to look like wood. Fiddling about inside with a magnet trying to find a lost nut, he was startled when the magnet flew out of his hand and stuck to the 'wooden' panel.

I had the occasional dodgy moment which I suppose was inevitable. At one period we were having trouble with steering arms on HKs fitted with power steering. We came to the conclusion that too much force was being applied to them on full lock, so I had two polished steel distance pieces made up and these were inserted in each end of the ram to restrict the movement. We fitted the modified ram to one of our own cars and I set off to test it. I had covered about ten miles and everything seemed in order until I took a fairly sharp left hand bend when the ram locked up, the steering wouldn't straighten and I went through a hedge, fortunately a soft one. We found hydraulic pressure had forced oil past the distance pieces causing a build-up which prevented the ram returning. Had it been a wall instead of a hedge or if I had been on right lock it could have been serious. We cut two grooves in the distance pieces to allow the oil to return and, not without a certain amount of misgiving, I tried it again. Everything was fine and we subsequently fitted them to all the power steering cars.

At various times I have been asked what it was like demonstrating cars like the Facel. As a rule it was enjoyable. It can first of all be said that the best part of the job was the journey to the prospective buyer, the slap-up lunch we usually had and the ride home after having made a sale. The demo itself was sometimes a period of extreme nervousness and, occasionally, unmitigated terror. It must be remembered that in 1959-64 the Facel was probably the fastest car on the road and its silent, effortless performance made the speed deceptive. Furthermore, motorways were only just beginning to appear, so the demos were all carried out on ordinary roads.

My own Facel 184 HYL photographed with a matching companion taken at a Club meeting near Salisbury.

Some of the purchasers were experienced fast motorists, some I already knew and, with strangers, a few discreet enquiries about their previous cars, etc., would be sufficient to inspire confidence. With these people I could sit and relax as I am not by nature a nervous passenger (I even go out with my wife!), but if they had just won the Pools and their previous car was a Morris Oxford, then I was in trouble!

I can recall a few dodgy drivers. One of them was a certain Lincolnshire farmer, well-known for his aggressive nature. He drove round the narrow lanes near his home like a madman, his young son in the back urging him on with cries of, "Come on Dad, let's see how fast it will go". Dad responded nobly and by the grace of God nothing came the other way. He bought one and proudly boasted to me that he would break it in six months. In fact it was two years before anything went wrong, when 3rd gear lost a few teeth. Not uncommon at the time. He then had the cheek to say he wanted a free replacement, so I reminded him of his boast, and charged him an extra tenner.

Another time I had to take an HK up to Lancashire for a titled lady to try. She drove it with skill and, on a busy fast road nearby, I thought rather recklessly. I wasn't too worried about it, but afterwards she said she would have one but could not buy it yet as she had recently had three bad smashes and thought she was going to lose her licence over the last one. She was also in trouble with her insurance company, so perhaps I hadn't been so safe after all!

On another occasion I had to demonstrate a Facel 2 to a doctor in Rochester Hospital. He turned out to be an Asian, very charming and the owner of a Mk 9 Jaguar. This was a promising start, so off we went.

We soon found ourselves on a newly-opened section of the M2, and down went his foot. Very shortly I noticed a funeral procession in the nearside lane some way ahead. The last car was a black Rover 90 and somehow it didn't seem to fit. Driving fast cars for a living, one develops a sort of instinct for potential hazards. I felt it possible the Rover was not part of the funeral and therefore might pull out to overtake. No such thought occurred to my Asian friend and he kept his foot hard down. Of course, the Rover did pull out to overtake, and the resultant antics of the Facel as he braked hard at around a hundred gave me visions of joining our mate in the front carriage of the funeral.

There was also the time when a young man who drove his XK150 with considerable abandon wanted his father to have an Excellence. He drove during the demo and although he drove very well he appeared to forget the car was about a foot wider than his Jaguar. I spent most of the trip working out the cost of putting a new side in an Excellence.

Another Excellence demonstration involved a gent in the West Country who had a chauffeur and he insisted he was to take the wheel. The chauffeur was a docile little man in his late fifties and he approached the car with the enthusiasm of a man about to enter a cage full of hungry lions! He obviously hadn't driven anything like it before – the press button gear selector had him foxed for a start – and the drive that followed must have been the most miserable he had ever experienced. He was conscious of his guv'nor's critical eye in the back and my presence in the front by his side probably didn't help either. I did my best to put him at his ease, but he gripped the steering wheel as if he was strangling his mother-in-law and the car weaved all over the place.

Looking back, it was good fun and I think we did well to sell the number of cars we did. It was not an easy task to get them established – for one thing they were expensive, insurance on them wasn't easy and people had to be convinced the cars would do all we said they would do. Abecassis and I did all the demos. It was fortunate we were both used to high speed driving and could exploit the performance of the cars without frightening the punters. We were also prepared to go anywhere at any time. We sold one car to a man a few hundred miles away, who told us afterwards he had approached two other high-performance car people. Both gave him the, 'We will call in next time we are in the area' routine, but when he telephoned us we took a car to him the next day. He had almost made up his mind before we got there.

During the Facel production years I must have covered many thousands of miles in them, mostly in HK500s. A lot of these miles were long daily trips in the course of a normal day's work and a lot were done on the continent.

It says much for the cars that when it occurred to me that some of these trips might be of interest, I realised they were so uneventful that there was little to write about. I suppose the worst trip was when I collected the cars for the 1961 Motor Show. This was always a nerve-racking time – our Show followed on immediately after the Paris Salon and, as very often the same cars were on display in both exhibitions, we could not collect them until the Paris Show had ended. Even when they were not the same cars we still had to wait as all the sales personnel were tied up with running their Stand and we could get little sense out of them.

The drill was that I flew over on the Sunday with one of HWM's staff, picked up the cars on Monday morning, drove to Le Touquet and went straight to Earls Court from Lydd where they were cleaned up ready for the press day on Tuesday. This was cutting things a bit fine and left no room for anything to go wrong.

On this particular occasion, Sunday dawned with thick fog. We groped our way to Heathrow, although there was obviously no chance of taking

Facel Vegas at a meeting of the French Facel Club the "Amicale" at Le Touquet in 1981. Attended by me and many other members of the British FVOC.

Another view of the Le Touquet gathering. The wonderful food presented is remembered as much as (if not more than) the splendid motor cars although the wine may have had something to do with it.

off then; but we hoped it might clear later on. It did not do so and we hung about all day, the place literally seething with people all doing the same thing. Finally they announced there would be no flying that day, so it was back home for a quick meal and a wash and up to the station to catch the boat train at Victoria.

There were, of course, hundreds of people on the train and boat – all the normal passengers plus the Heathrow and Gatwick frustrated airline passengers. There was no possibility of a sleep on the boat; we just dozed in chairs while we crept along, fog horn blowing all the time. There was considerable confusion at Boulogne with a few bleary-eyed Customs men quite unprepared for such an invasion, but finally we were on the train to Paris.

It was two very weary and travel-stained bods that arrived at the Gare du Nord in the early hours of the morning. Fortunately, French railway stations are much more civilised than their English counterparts, so we were able to clean up and have a decent meal whilst waiting for the Facel office to open. We took a taxi to the office, arriving just after nine. Of course, no-one was ready for us, and there was no sign of the cars. Eventually the paperwork was sorted out, the cars arrived and we were ready to go.

We had three cars to collect. One of them was a black Excellence, the last one we were to get although we didn't know it at the time. It was a big improvement on the others and was already sold, the purchaser having kindly given us permission to put it on the Show stand. The other two consisted of a Facellia and the lhd Facel 2 taken off the stand at the Paris Salon. I took the Excellence, my colleague drove the Facellia and one of Facel's senior staff, M. Latham, brought the Facel 2. This car was only on loan to us for the Show and therefore came into the UK (and was exported from France) on temporary papers. It was easier and likely to cause less aggro at the Customs if driven by a Frenchman.

It was still foggy as we groped our way out of Paris. We took my usual route instead of the recognised way via St Denis, which brought one onto the N.1 just north of the City. By going directly North I could divert quite easily to the service dept. at Puteaux and the factory at Colombes, something I frequently had to do. On this occasion I had no calls to make, but in the fog it was better to go the way I knew so well, joining the N.1 just south of Beauvais.

At Méru we were held up at a level crossing and I got out to see if the others were OK. To my surprise I found three cars had joined our convoy – two of them English. It transpired that they had been trying to find their way out of Paris in the fog, spotted us, guessed where we were heading and tagged along. They stayed with us until we reached Beauvais and then disappeared into the gloom.

It was well into the afternoon when we reached Le Touquet, only to find more confusion. The fog had only just cleared enough at Lydd to commence flying and everyone was milling around trying to get a flight.

Three pictures of the Facel Vega Owners Club Stand at the Birmingham Classic Car Show. For such a small club (small in membership although the size of the cars makes up for it), it wasn't a bad effort.

As they normally stopped flying at dusk, I was pretty pessimistic about our chances. However, I had got to knew them all very well and they rallied round in fine style. Whilst Silver City organised me a special plane, Cyril Collier (the RAC representative) took all the papers along to the Customs and got them stamped in record time. We took off just before dusk and arrived at Lydd just as the weather clamped down again. The Customs at Lydd were also very helpful, but even so it was dark and getting late when we eventually left for home.

The fog had turned into a thick rainy mist, the journey was dead miserable and seemed endless. The poor Frenchman had a shocking ride – he had no idea where he was, so had to keep me in his sights all the time. It was dark, misty and drizzling, he had yellow headlamps which dipped to the right and he was on the wrong side of the road. We arrived at HWM about eleven o'clock. I unlocked the workshop and thankfully put the cars away. My eyes were out on stalks through peering through the mist, I hadn't slept for 42 hours and the strain of leading the convoy all day and half the night, knowing it was vital the cars were not damaged in the fog, was considerable.

I had telephoned Hilda from Lydd to warn her we were having a Frenchman to stay the night, as it was obvious he would not get to the hotel he had booked in London. She was a bit apprehensive, being one of those people who thinks anyone born outside the UK must be either a Zulu or a Red Indian! When I presented M. Latham, an educated, very charming gentleman who I knew quite well, she was most relieved and no longer feared having her throat cut in the night.

I telephoned Abecassis at the hotel he used in London during the Show, much to his relief. He arranged for the cars to be cleaned next morning and taken up to Earls Court, where they arrived about mid-day. I went to bed and stayed there for many hours, arriving at the Show late afternoon to see my precious cargo all shiny and surrounded by admiring pressmen and traders.

Little did they know how near they had been to seeing an empty Stand! I was sorry when the Facel went out of production. A new model with a more modern chassis was in the pipeline but never came to fruition. My association with it had broadened my experience and I had met some charming people. I got to know and love Paris and have gone back there twice a year ever since. The Patron, M. Jean Daninos, is still around; now a sprightly 80 year old, he travels widely selling a sort of Portuguese Land Rover. When he is in London we meet for a meal and when I am in Paris I try to see him.

Some people never learn and around 1963 we started all over again with the Iso Rivolta, which I will cover in the next chapter.

7

The Iso Rivolta

I cannot remember now how we came to get involved with Iso. It was somehow connected with Samango Turner, head of Yeoman Credit, who ran a racing car team at the time. He was either Italian or had Italian connections and I recall a lunch at a hotel near London Airport with him, Abecassis, myself and two people from Iso, one being Bizzarini the designer. As a result we took up the concession.

It is natural to compare the Iso with the Facel. Both had the same idea of an American V8 engine in a continental chassis, both were the brainchild of one man – Daninos with the Facel and Count Rivolta with the Iso. Both were built in already established industrial complexes presided over by the forenamed gentlemen.

In reality the two cars were very different. Each had its attractions and it is difficult to say one was better than the other. The Facel was more solid, nicer inside, quieter and generally gave more luxurious motoring. Moreover, it looked worth the £5000 or so price tag that it carried. On the other hand the Iso was lighter in weight and controls, more responsive, had a much nicer gearbox and clutch and could be driven with more abandon on twisty roads.

Specification was fairly orthodox: the engine a 90° V8 Chevrolet Corvette, of 5359 cc with a compression ratio of 10.5 to 1. Two versions were available, one giving 300 bhp at 5000 rpm and the other 340 bhp at 6000 rpm. Front suspension was coil and wishbone, many of the parts being of UK origin. Rear suspension used the De Dion axle layout with coil springs. The rear axle was by Salisbury with ratios of 3.07 or 2.88 to 1. Dunlop disc brakes all round took care of retardation.

This is the first Iso Rivolta to arrive in the UK. The photograph shows it at Le Touquet Airport awaiting a flight on my return from the visit to the factory at Bresso, near Milan. I had my best ever run across France on this occasion. Apologies for the poor quality of the picture but it is the only one I have of a memorable occasion.

The body was by Bertone and followed the Italian style of the day. It was reasonably well-finished, good by Italian standards but lacked the luxury and opulence of the Facel.

The background of the car is more obscure to me than that of the Facel. The factory was large, modern and very clean with the car production separate from their other activities. What these were I never really knew except for the manufacture of a cunning little three-wheeled truck called the Isocarro. This had a single front wheel steered direct which looked like the front assembly of a scooter. A tiny 148.7cc engine was under the seat for which they claimed 7 bhp at 5000 rpm! In unit with the engine was a four speed gearbox, an open propeller shaft delivering the power to an ordinary live axle.

The first car arrived in, I think, 1963. It was sent over by rail and I collected it from a goods yard off the Old Kent Road. Having completed the paper work I was given the keys, climbed aboard the flat truck and switched on. The engine burst into life but stopped before I could reverse off. Either the Italians had been extremely clever in working out the petrol required to get it to the train or it had been milked en route.

Railway staff at that time were quite helpful, not yet having attended a course on 'How to be bloody minded without trying'. A gang of lads pushed me off into a corner and told me where I could get a can of petrol. Their optimism proved ill-founded and it was many weary minutes later when I arrived back with enough to get me to a garage. Having got home, I inspected the car thoroughly as we still knew very little about them and proceeded to run it in. At this stage I had not been to the factory and seen the belting the engines got on the test bench or I wouldn't have bothered. The more I drove it the more I disliked it. Performance was electrifying, albeit with plenty of noise. Iso claimed a standing kilometre time of under 28 seconds and this was almost certainly justified. What we could not reach however was their claimed 148 mph maximum. At about 115 it started to falter and dried up completely at 120.

The factory professed to be surprised, saying they never had problems. As they were within a few minutes of an Autostrada and as their test drivers were much braver and/or more foolish than Abecassis and myself, we felt they must be telling the truth and that our car was at fault. It felt like fuel starvation so as a first step I fitted a twin electric pump into the line with a separate switch. When the engine started to falter we cut the extra pump in but it made no difference. I tried everything else: a high speed coil, different plugs, experimented with different carburettor, jets etc., but to no avail. Suddenly I remembered something that should have struck me before.

In the old Aston Martin days we had similar trouble when the 3-litre engine replaced the 2.6 in the DB 2/4, particularly when on reserve. It turned out to be the main fuel pipe which had too small a bore, the head of petrol reaching the engine being insufficient for the increased power of the 3-litre unit. Examination of the Iso pipe showed it to be quite small so I reckoned I had found the answer. Before I could do anything about it we had a call from the factory. They admitted the trouble, said they had found the answer and would I take our car over for this and one or two other modifications.

A trip to Milan was not to be missed so off I went.

After a very pleasant trip through France and Switzerland, I put the car on the train to go through the Simplon tunnel. It would have been nicer to have driven over the pass but the train was so much quicker and, being early April, there was some doubt as to whether the pass could be negotiated. The run through Italy was uneventful and next day I reported at the factory in Bresso. The car was whisked away and two mechanics immediately started working on it.

During the days that followed I was allowed to roam about the works as much as I liked, but for some reason was not allowed to go near our own car so had no idea what they were doing to it. The most impressive thing at Bresso was the engine test bed. Whether they did anything to the engines or whether they were standard. I was never able to find out, but the row of engines waiting to go on the rig and the thorough, precise way they were tested was worthy of Enzo Ferrari at his best.

In a separate partitioned-off corner I came across Bizzarini working on a car he had entered for Le Mans. This was a beautiful looking car, low, sleek and purposeful, and he called it a Grifo. No attempt had been made to attain a high standard of finish, there was no interior trim, window

The first Grifo. This one was produced by Bizzarini at the Iso factory in Bresso and collected by me from Milan airport. It had electrifying performance but very few concessions to silence and comfort.

mechanism, etc; everything has been done for lightness and a determination by Bizzarini that it should hold together for 24 hours. It duly ran at Le mans and, although well down in the results, it did finish after a trouble-free run, no mean achievement for a one off entry. Bizzarini spoke no English but I gathered I was welcome to look around and even hand him the odd spanner. I was also told a slightly more civilised version was to be made to sell to the public.

Meanwhile our car was being put together again and by mid-week it was ready for test, but it still dried up at speed. I mentioned my theory of too small a fuel pipe but they felt this was not the answer. Two days later they announced the trouble had been cured and the head tester asked me to go with him to try it. Having experienced a previous test run with this gentleman, I made the excuse of a headache and said I would try it myself in the morning. As soon as the commuter traffic to Milan had cleared next day I took it on the Autostrada and was able to hold an indicated 140mph for about two thirds of a kilometre. All was now well.

They did not tell me what they had done and it was not until I got home and put the car on the hoist that I discovered a new fuel pipe of considerably larger bore than the original. Like the French, they could not bring themselves to admit we were sometimes as clever as they were.

The run home itself was fabulous. Leaving Bresso after lunch I again took the train through the Simplon, having just time before embarking to flog my tourist petrol coupons on the black market. Reaching the Swiss-French border in the early evening I crossed over and spent the night at Pontarlier a few miles on the French side. Leaving there at 6 a.m. next morning, I reached Le Touquet in the early afternoon having made one stop for petrol. A quick lunch at the Airport whilst waiting for my flight and I was home for my evening meal. The whole trip from the Swiss border to Walton took just 13 hours and I can think of no other car that would have made it so easy.

We then proceeded to use the car for demonstrations, personal transport and for experimental purposes, much as we had done with our Facel Vegas. Commercially it was not a success. We sold one or two but, superb performer that it undoubtedly was, it still failed to make a significant impact. I suppose there were several reasons for this but the main one was probably because it didn't look worth the high asking price. Compared with the Facel it was very ordinary; although quite handsome it looked little different from any other Bertone bodied car of the period. The interior lacked an 'expensive look' even though leather was used for the upholstery. Moreover, it was noisy. Be that as it may, it was an exciting car to drive and deserved better success. The next big event in the Iso story was the news that our first Grifo was ready. By this time Bizzarini was making them independently of the Iso organisation, but using their works and marketing facilities.

I flew over to Milan to collect it and it was waiting at the Airport, low and rakish, painted in bright red. Two Iso mechanics were there with another car and suggested I follow them to the factory. I got in and found I could not see a thing. To get the low roof line the seats were bolted directly to the floor with no runners, the seat and squab had only an inch of padding and I sat so low I could not see over the steering wheel. The rear window was in the horizontal part of the tail making the mirror useless, and I could not reach the pedals.

I emptied my overnight bag, sat on my pyjamas, spare shirt, etc., and stuffed the bag behind my back. I wasn't much help but the best I could do. Meanwhile the two Italians had shot off and I was left to find my own way across Milan. With only the vaguest idea of which way to go I set off and eventually saw a sign pointing to the Milan-Turin autostrada. Once I

Another view of the same car in its standard form as issued from the factory. Both these photographs were taken at Walton-on-Thames

found that I knew I would be alright so I pressed on hoping there would be more signs further on. The trip through the city remains a nightmare to this day. Barely able to see, hardly reaching the pedals and not knowing the way, I floundered on, receiving no mercy from the natives who naturally expected an Italian sports car on Italian number plates to be driven flat out. Somehow I made the autostrada without mishap and eventually reached the factory.

After dealing with the paperwork I set off home, having already decided to take my time in view of the uncomfortable driving position. With memories of the pleasant two days Hilda and I spent in Stresa back in 1950, I decided to make it my overnight stop and pulled into the same hotel about tea time. The car had been a sensation all the way. No-one seemed to know what it was and many a minor shunt was narrowly averted as other drivers got too close in order to look. A big crowd surrounded it as I pulled into the hotel forecourt, asking questions and surprised I could not answer them, once more being foxed by the Italian number plates. Fearing for its safety I stuffed a handful of lira into the fist of one of the hotel porters and asked him to look after it.

Soon bathed and refreshed I was eating an excellent meal, complemented by a bottle of Ruffino. The view over Lake Maggiore was superb, the lights along the edge of the lake, the music and the delightful atmosphere of the place made the frustrations of the day and the problems of the morrow insignificant.

Next morning I went to the car fully expecting it to be stripped by souvenir hunters, as obviously my porter friend could not have guarded it all night. It was quite intact and I concluded that Italy was the same as Britain and other European countries in that the people outside the big cities were of a different character to those within. Before setting off I purchased some inflatable cushions and some webbing. With these strapped to the seat and squab I could see where I was going, could reach the pedals and no longer felt every bump in the road through my backside. My position thus transformed, I set about enjoying the performance of the car – and what a performance it was! There was only one word for it, shattering! In the past I had driven examples of practically every fast car made, I had raced and test-driven formula one single seaters and competition sports cars, but had never experienced anything like it. Some two years later *The Autocar* tested a production and much more civilised version made by Iso and they were lyrical in their report on its performance. Our car was lighter and, with no attempt at mechanical refinement, it went like the proverbial rocket.

Again using the Simplon tunnel, I drove fairly sedately through Switzerland in deference to the road conditions and the feelings of the local populace but, once clear of the mountains on the French side, the long straight roads were an open invitation. When I put my foot down the rev counter shot round so rapidly I felt the clutch must be slipping, but it wasn't. Maximum speeds were 80 mph in first, 106 in second, 132 in third and 165 in top. These were speedometer readings but a subsequent check proved they were not far out. The acceleration matched these figures and the general sensation was out of this world. The whole business was accompanied by all the authentic Italian noises: the valve gear clattered, the exhaust crackled and the suspension thumped away with gusto. Of course the very low roof line and lack of substantial interior trim accentuated the noise and it became tiring after a while. The car was completely lacking in temperament, so it was possible to drive it in a reasonably docile manner and for the most part I did, but had plenty of fun when I felt like it.

One of my favourite ways of enlivening the journey was to catch up a Frenchman who thought he was shifting, change down and overtake him at about 120 mph nonchalantly changing up when level enough for him to see me do it. I stuck to my resolution to take my time, stopping at some of the more interesting towns and cities to look around and to indulge in one of my favourite pastimes, looking over old churches and cathedrals.

This view shows the Grifo after essential modifications to the design of the rear window; carried out by the factory at our request. This shot was taken "somewhere in France" on the way back from the factory. Now we had a better chance of seeing what was following us, even though they never seemed to get very close.

Arriving home eventually, we set about making the car more suitable for everyday motoring but, although partially successful, it was obvious it was only going to sell on its performance, and that for refined fast motoring the Facel was still top dog. We then lent it to *The Autocar* who intended giving it a full road test, but after a few days it was returned, a sheepish Ronald Barker announcing that it felt funny at the back and was making a lot of noise. I took it out and within a few yards decided that Ron was one of the greatest masters of understatement I had met – it was virtually undriveable. A glance over my shoulder revealed the top ends of the telescopic rear dampers poking up into the rear compartment and waving about like flags. The body had in fact completely broken away at the point where the shock absorbers were mounted. This was an obvious weakness so I made up different mountings arc-welded to a more substantial part of the monocoque and these proved to be satisfactory.

At this point it seemed prudent to experiment with Selectarides so I took the car to my friends at Fulford, where we tried out different settings as we had with the Facel. This had been on the agenda for some time, mostly because of the vast capacity of the petrol tank. It held 37 gallons and in those days one could afford to fill it. This was a considerable weight and the handling varied noticeably according to whether the tank was full or down to the last few gallons, so some method of compensating seemed desirable.

The car ran trouble free for about 5000 miles and then needed a new clutch, probably because the load on it was more than it was designed to take. Shortly after this we were informed by Bizzarini that they had altered the shape of the rear end to give better visibility through the rear window and he offered to alter our car if we cared to send it over. This was a desirable modification and as Abecassis was due to go on holiday to the south of France he dropped it in at Bresso on the way.

Some time later I flew over to pick it up and there was no doubt it was a vast improvement. Once more I set off on the long trek home, this time much more comfortably. I decided to try the recently opened St. Bernard tunnel as one could drive through instead of having to take the train. It was most impressive; the engineering was superb with both Italian and Swiss Customs posts in the middle. The only drama of the trip occurred when I entered Switzerland. Like most people leaving Italy I had put the minimum quantity of petrol necessary to get me to the border, it being much cheaper in Switzerland. I stopped at the first petrol station I saw to fill up. The attendant commenced operations and was busy squirting away when a shout went up from a passer by. Dashing round to the other side of the car I saw petrol starting to leak onto the forecourt. This was obviously a dangerous situation, so I dammed the flow, the proprietor emptied his sand buckets and I drove off using plenty of revs in order to bring the fuel level down to below the source of the leak as quickly as possible. Fortunately, it was a scorching hot day so the trail of petrol I left on the road quickly evaporated.

Coming to a village I pulled into the local garage and explained my plight. We put the car over a pit and found the reason. The Grifo tank was divided into three sections, one each side and one on top with a common filler cap in the top tank. When filling it gravitated to the side tanks first and then filled the top one. It took little time to discover the connecting pipe between the two side tanks was missing and this had not come to light in Italy because I was below the level of the outlets. My garage friend offered to make up a pipe by ten the following morning so I booked into the village hotel, a charming, typically Swiss establishment, where I was soon enjoying a locally caught trout, beautifully cooked in wine. Next morning I went round to the garage. The car was still over the pit so I got down, looked underneath and found he had made up a new pipe. The whole job was beautifully done, the charge was reasonable so I made his day by filling up with 160 litres of petrol.

I was in no great hurry to get back so stopped off in Geneva for a few hours and stayed the night near the border. Next day I made my way via Dôle, Dijon, Avallon and Auxerre to Paris. Being reluctant to leave the car in the street all night, I left it at the Facel works with a list of parts I wished to take back in the morning. These were waiting for me when I arrived around 10 o'clock and, after a few minutes delay whilst the paper work was completed, I set off for Le Touquet.

I was about 5 kilometres from Etaples when two policemen stepped into the road and waved me into the side. Naturally, I wondered what I had done, my first thought being that I had been speeding through a village and they had been contacted over the radio. They went through the motions, checked my papers and Green Card, but I soon realised they had stopped me because they were intrigued with the car, never having seen one before. I played along with them (one does with French policemen!), let them look all over it and opened the bonnet. I have no idea what they expected to see but it certainly wasn't a crude-looking American V8 and their disappointment was obvious. I arrived home in the evening after a thoroughly enjoyable trip.

The new rear window treatment was a great improvement and we set about trying to sell some cars. It was an impossibly task, really. The car was too crude, too fast and quite impractical. We managed to sell one, but I cannot remember now who bought it. George Abecassis used it as his personal transport and I imagine it became well known on the route between his home in Marlow and Walton-on-Thames. I drove it frequently myself particularly to motor race meetings where I could show it off in the paddock.

At that time the Hants. and Berks. MC held a meeting once a year where we all gathered at one of the local pubs. People who owned or had access to interesting cars brought them along to give demonstrations. A short rectangular course was mapped out which included a length of de-restricted dual carriageway and several interesting corners. I had attended for several years with Aston Martin and Facel Vega and had always been kept very busy. The night I took the Grifo they were queuing for rides the whole time. Everyone wanted to experience 80 in first, 100 in second, and 130 in third. I never got into top. These were wonderful evenings; the Police co-operated and the local residents thoroughly enjoyed it, standing at their gates and waving. For our part, we acted responsibly, only went fast where it was safe to do so, respected little built-up areas and did not carve up other traffic. It is sad to think it could not happen today.

Not long afterwards we sold the Grifo and gave up the concession, which was taken up by Trojan Cars at Croydon.

By this time Count Rivolta and Bizzarini had settled their differences and produced the Iso Grifo. This was a beautiful car, the same basic shape and mechanics but with comfortable seats, full trim and carpets, electric windows, etc. Performance was not as electrifying as the original but still better than most. *The Autocar* tested one in 1966 and recorded a best top speed of 163 mph. They described it as a dream car come true which about sums it up.

We had one ourselves and sold several more, but soon after this I left HWM and to my regret have not driven one since. Both the Facel and the Iso were notable cars and, although these days I am mostly concerned with more mundane vehicles, I can look back with pleasure, feeling happy that I have left my mark on two outstanding cars of the period.

8
FIFTY YEARS OF JAGUARS

It is probably true to say my Jaguar story began in October 1931 when I opened my show number of *The Motor* and found inside a description of a sensational new sports coupé. It was very low with a long louvred bonnet, close fitting wings and knock-on wire wheels. Built on a Standard 16 chassis, specially adapted, it was called the SS and made by the Swallow Coachbuilding Co. I couldn't wait for Saturday when I was going to Olympia and made a beeline for the Swallow stand as soon as I got in. I sat in the car and decided it was the car for me when I got rich.

As it happened I never even drove one. They had a very limited market, being virtually a two seater, but it wasn't long before they were given a four seater body with long flowing wings and running boards. This model was much more practical, sold quite well, and it wasn't long before I got my hands on one. It was still a coupé; the rear quarters were leather covered with dummy pram irons in the fashion of the day and the rear seats were like two armchairs.

At that time the garage was owned by three partners. One of them was a dapper little man, full of fun, a great liking and capacity for beer and women, and a huge fund of dirty stories. We all thought the world of him. He knew nothing about motor cars, garages or business generally and was there because a) he had money in it, and b) he was the Chairman's brother-in-law. When you think about it, two jolly good reasons!

One day he came in, grinning from ear to ear, driving a very smart SSi open tourer. It looked a picture – dark red with polished discs on the wheels and red trim. He had just bought it and handed it over to me for a road test and check over. It was in very good shape, but the engine smoked a bit and a few weeks use confirmed it was using oil.

In due course I took the engine out and stripped it, finding very little wear in bores or bearings, so decided new rings and a valve grind would bring it back to scratch. At this stage I had an idea, for I was a crafty little sod in those days and wanted the car for a trip I had in mind. I assembled the engine with minimum clearances and it was obviously tight. I then regaled him with the strict necessity of running it in carefully: no more than 2500 rpm, not to let it labour, keep a strict eye on the temperature and oil pressure gauges, etc. I knew he had neither the patience nor the skill to do all this, so he asked me to run it in for him. With an air of doing him a great favour I agreed, had a lovely week or so, and then did my trip. In fairness I ran it in most carefully and, before handing it back, spent a long time setting up the two RAG carburettors and checking it over. It ran as sweet as a nut and never used a pint of oil as long as we had it.

I drove quite a lot of these SSIs, including many miles in a 20 hp Airline, and enjoyed them all, also one or two SSIIs. By the end of 1934 the coupé had been made into a four light saloon and was a much nicer car, although still two door.

In September 1935 the SS Jaguar was announced with ohv engine, and very good looking coachwork. I must admit that on this occasion my crystal ball let me down as I felt it would not be able to compete with the new 2 litre MG announced about the same time. We were MG distributors at the time and soon sold several 2-litres, some of which I collected from Abingdon myself. However, my opinion was altered when I drove my first SS Jaguar – it was a much better car.

The seven bearing crankshaft made it much smoother than the MG, the driving position was superb and it handled like a thoroughbred. The Girling brakes, operated by rods in tension, were very good but did not compare with the Lockheed hydraulic system on the MG and this was probably the only feature where the latter scored.

It took Jaguar some time to get down to hydraulic brakes. The SSI had the dreadful Bendix cable operated, self-energising system. Although extremely powerful they were a nightmare to maintain. It would take ages to get them properly balanced and then one emergency stop would leave them pulling all over the road.

I enjoyed quite a bit of Jaguar motoring, particularly liking the $3\frac{1}{2}$-litre model and the SS100. It was said the latter was unstable at speed due to wind getting under the wings. I never knew whether this was fact or theory and can only say I drove them as fast as I could, and it never happened to me, so I do not know at what speed it came in.

Here at Lands End is one of my favourite Jaguars, VLB7, a 3.4 Mk.1. This beautiful car was my personal transport for many years and was as much at home flat out on the long French Autoroutes as when shopping locally. This model always reminds me of the great days of saloon car racing with Mike Hawthorn and his peers dicing around those circuits sideways-on in a tradition that has now vanished.

After the war I was able to enjoy more Jaguar motoring. Stephen had an American uncle who was able to buy one of the first post-war 3½-litre saloons off the export quota. It was rhd and kept over here for his use on visits to the UK. As these were not very frequent I used it a lot to keep it in good trim. I couldn't drive it as much as I would have liked as I could hardly use his petrol coupons and there was a limit to how much I could fiddle, even in my job. Nevertheless, when I wanted something bigger or posher than my own 6-cylinder Wolseley Hornet coupé it was nearly always available.

I drove many others Jaguars, including the Mk V introduced in the latter part of 1948. I thought it a nice car, but somehow lacked the character of the Mk IV, as it became known.

Then, at the 1948 Show, appeared what was probably the biggest sensation to hit the motoring world, the XK 120. Here was a car with magnificent twin ohc engine capable of 160 bhp at 5000 rpm, modern front suspension, a very high standard of interior trim and instrumentation and the whole lot enclosed in a body of breathtaking beauty. There could be no doubt about the performance and it was not long before this was confirmed in record breaking and competition.

I reckoned I would soon get a drive in one. Most of the racing drivers of the day were frequent visitors to HWM. I felt pretty sure they would get some of the first cars and they were always happy to let me try their

Two views of VLB7 on a local run with Jimpy our German Shepherd and in the heathland of the New Forest. It didn't take much to persuade me to take the dog for a walk a hundred miles from home with a car like that to get there.

cars. I was not disappointed and can still remember my first drive. Out of the window went previous ideas that a sports car had to be noisy and uncomfortable. This car was fast, quiet and equally happy in heavy traffic as it was on the open road.

There were no disc brakes then and the biggest problem was brake fade. On the road it was not too apparent, but on two occasions I tested them at Goodwood. I found it very disconcerting to have the brakes deteriorating all round the circuit and then arrive at the chicane with none at all. I know the Stirling Mosses and Salvadoris of this world can lap as fast without brakes as with them, but I guess I was cast in a different mould. The XK 140 which followed was an improved car in many ways, but somehow seemed to lack the fine balance of the 120. It still had drum brakes, but was fitted with rack and pinion steering which gave you more chance of not hitting anything when you ran out of brakes.

It was a superb car and is probably the most collectable today. John Heath had one which was tweaked a bit and I much enjoyed driving it. I don't think I am alone in thinking its successor, the XK 150, was nowhere near as nice, disc brakes notwithstanding. Stephen had one and neither of us liked it much. It was still a good car and terrific value but it felt heavier and I thought the high scuttle spoilt the lines.

By this time we were Jaguar agents, so when new models came out I was able to sample them and also got involved in other Jaguar activities.

The Mk VII introduced in 1950 was a very fine car although it didn't reach UK buyers for some time. With the XK engine, beautiful lines and sumptuous interior, it was incredible value for money. There can be little doubt that this car and its successors, the M Type, Mk VIII and Mk IX sounded the death knell for firms like Armstrong Siddeley, Alvis, etc. Had I been in the market for this type of car there is no question that the Jaguar would have been my choice, but to show how things alter with the years, I have owned a 3-litre Alvis for some time and wouldn't swap it now for a contemporary Jaguar.

I was very pleased to make my own small contribution to the Mk VII series. We had a favoured customer who always had the first of a new model. One of them – after all this time I cannot remember which – got water in the left hand tank the first time the car was washed. On taking out the boot trim we found Jaguars had altered the breather pipe so that it fed into the drain pipe from the filler cap nacelle. On this car the pipe was trapped by its securing clip so that water drained from the nacelle into the breather, and then into the tank. I made a mod to overcome this and, rather with tongue in cheek, wrote to Jaguar giving them a drawing illustrating the fault.

I received a charming letter from Geoffrey Pindar saying they had checked all the cars on the floor and found seven of them with the same fault. He was most grateful.

This was the start of a sort of pen and telephone friendship between us, although I did meet him on one of my visits to the factory. They were a great bunch of fellows in those days. Apart from Pindar I recall MacDonald and a few others. They were completely dedicated to Jaguar and must have been one of the finest service teams in the industry. They also had a first

The usual problems of securing supplies of spare parts for a limited production car
affected our business with Facel. There were many occasions when I had to dash to Paris
to collect vital bits and pieces to keep our customers happy. Here is VLB7 at Le
Touquet, its roofrack packed not with camping gear but "pièces de réchange". The Mk.1
had a balanced engine, wire wheels and all the features to make it a superb grand tourer.
I wish I had it still today.

rate team of travelling Service Engineers. These men were hand picked and superb. Apart from investigating unusual problems which arose from time to time, they made regular visits to dealers, spending the day with us. We were notified well in advance which gave me a chance to get in any problem cars, or customers who I knew would appreciate the opportunity to talk to a factory engineer. I always tried to strike a good balance between the moaners and know-alls and the pleasant types so that his day wasn't all aggro. To see these chaps in action was a treat; apart from their technical knowledge they were diplomats and the essence of charm. At lunch time we would go to the local pub for a pie and a pint. We would yarn and swap experiences and altogether it made a very pleasant day.

A typical example of the spirit prevailing then was the case of a man with a new Mk VII who wrote to the factory complaining his car used oil. He received a very nice reply saying it probably would at first, but would he write again at 10,000 miles.

Now this chap only used his car for commuting to the station a mile away and trips to the golf course at weekends of about the same distance.

Nevertheless he kept the letter and, nearly eight years later, wrote again saying he had now done 10,000 miles and it still used oil. Of course it was a leg pull, but he received a very nice letter back. They still had the original correspondence and were willing to help him. He never took them up on it and we all had a good laugh.

All those chaps, Pindar and his merry men, the Service Engineers, all seemed to disappear when Jaguar merged with BL, or whatever they were called in those days. I don't think many of them were retiring age, and feel it more likely they were disillusioned with the new set up.

Meanwhile the smaller cars were announced. We had one of the first 2.4 saloons and found it a very pleasant car, but somehow not quite what we expected. It was a much more handy size and one grew to like it, particularly when compared with the Armstrong Siddeley 236, Rover 90 and the like. It was naturally improved bit by bit, and the 3.4 with disc brakes was a fine car. I had one of these for about two years. It had belonged to a Coventry doctor and the engine had been specially balanced by the factory. With wire wheels, overdrive and disc brakes it was one of the best cars I've had. At this period we had taken up the Facel Vega Concession and I used to commute regularly to Paris in the 3.4 to sort out any problems and load up with spares for the return journey. It was an ideal car for the long French roads and never let me down. VLB 7, where are you now?

The Mk 2 was a big improvement and, as everyone knows, is now a Classic. Over the years I've had two of these and a Daimler version. One of these was a 3.4 with wire wheels and a high ratio back axle. It was a lovely car to drive and I wish I still had it.

In around 1962 Abecassis wanted to tow a very large cruiser on a four wheel trailer to Cannes and asked me to share the driving with him. We decided a 3.8 Mk 2 with automatic, power steering and wire wheels would be the ideal towing vehicle and duly purchased a good example. We drove off the Boulogne ferry about 6 in the evening and planned to drive through the night and the following day, taking it in turns to drive and sleep. We did this with no trouble at all, only stopping for petrol, meals and a wash, etc., arriving in Cannes at 7 pm the following evening. I've no idea of the distance, but it was a long way and it says a lot for the car that we were not tired.

I drove along the coast to the Victoria, a hotel I had used before which was very good and reasonably priced for that part of the world, and next morning set off for Paris. Not having a whacking great boat behind I took my favourite route via Grasse, Grenoble and Lyon, spent the night in Paris, the morning at the Facel works, caught the air ferry at Le Touquet late afternoon, and was home in the evening. It was a lot of motoring in three days, particularly towing a large boat on the outward trip, but the car never missed a beat and I couldn't have wished for anything better. I drove lots of other Mk 2s, both in the course of my job and for pleasure. One of our Facel Vega customers lived in Scotland. He used to change his cars very

Opposite top: *I had several Mk.2 Jaguars; this one finished in British Racing Green. When these cars were easy to find and not too expensive to buy we didn't treasure them as much as today's enthusiasts. This was a beautiful car and I consider myself mad to have sold it.*

Opposite bottom: *This is a favourite 'S' type. The 3.8 engine is fitted with automatic transmission which made it into a delightful, refined high speed touring car. The 'S' type was unappreciated for many years but is now much sought-after, with good reason. This photograph is taken at Aberdarron, North Wales.*

Another much underrated Jaguar is the 420. I thought them excellent particularly after Browns Lane had sorted out the gear ratios. This one also finished in my favourite British Racing Green was particularly cherished and photographed in Petworth Park, Sussex.

frequently and we got to know him quite well. As a result we started selling him Mk 2 Jaguars for his wife, also changed regularly. I would leave early, meet him in Carlisle, we would have lunch and then change over cars. The best route in those days was the A1 to Scotch Corner, across to Penrith and then the A6. It was a round trip of well over 600 miles, but by then the A1 was a good fast road and a 3.8 Mk 2 with automatic and power steering made light of it all.

For some time I used a 2.4 with overdrive which was a very pleasant car, lacking the poke of the larger engined cars but surprisingly fast on a long run once you got going.

I used a Mk 10 for a while, but felt it wasn't Jaguar's best effort and we had a fair bit of trouble with them.

I liked the S type and the 420 and have owned two of each. I think the 420 was, and possibly still is, very much underrated. When it first came out it seemed a bit gutless compared with the others. The 4.2 engine had a completely different power curve and the choice of gear ratios didn't help either. This was rectified early in the production run and the second one I had was an extremely nice car.

Meanwhile the E-type came on the market, and I drove quite a number. I liked them and, when the 4.2 was produced with a better gearbox and other improvements, Stephen bought one. We had a lot of fun with it and very little trouble, except with door and tailgate locks.

By the time the XJ6 appeared I had left HWM and started my own business, still specialising in Jaguars. I felt the XJ would be out of my reach for some years, but one day I was visiting a pal of mine who ran a Volvo agency and in his car park was a rather dejected looking XJ6 4.2. He told me he had taken it in, wasn't very interested in it, and offered it to me at a price which was reasonable for a car that was difficult to get. I left my 420 there, and drove the XJ back to my garage. It was beautiful on the road and close examination revealed it only needed a little care and attention to make a nice car.

Next day, after a bit of haggling, it was mine, the first of nine XJ6s I was to own. There really is nothing to touch them for effortless, comfortable motoring.

One day I called on Gavin Fairfax, Rover dealers at Virginia Water, who were old friends of mine. In the car park was a 1948 2½-litre Jaguar, looking a bit sorry for itself but complete. I asked who it belonged to and was told the Sales Manager. Two days later I received a 'phone call from him. He had got the sack and had to remove the Jaguar immediately and would I buy it? Under the circumstances it was going cheap so another wreck joined the outfit. I did some dismantling myself, had some chrome done and overhauled various items. The following year I sent it to the Isle of Wight, on a trailer, where they took the body off. They overhauled the engine and chassis, I got a new exhaust system through the Jaguar Drivers' Club, and it all progressed very well until we came to the body. It proved impossible to get anyone to come to our premises and do all the metalwork. Neither did they want the body taken to their workshops as they like to be able to push things about as it suits them. I got fed up with all the aggro so when a local lad made a good offer for it as it stood, I let him have it and have often regretted it. I've never counted it as one of my cars as I never drove it.

After a succession of second-hand ones I was able to achieve a life's ambition and buy a brand-new Jaguar. It was to have been a great day for me, but on the day I got it our much loved alsatian died and the car meant nothing to me at all.

One day I heard on the grapevine that Jaguars were bringing out a two-door version. A visit to my friends at Lex Mead confirmed this and I signed an order form on the spot. In due course it was announced officially, but some months later Lex told me the 6-cylinder version was not going to be made. This seemed a bit odd so I wrote to the factory, who confirmed it.

This is the Jaguar of my life. I purchased this XJ6C new in 1977 and it is still in my possession having covered a mere 9500 miles. The two door coupé is fast becoming a classic and mine must be one of the best. In order not to raise false hopes I declare it not for sale . . .

It was typical of the attitude of both companies at the time that neither of them suggested I had a V12 instead. I liked the original carburettor V12 engine, and would certainly have done so but didn't feel it was up to me to suggest it. As everyone knows, they did bring out the 6, but again no-one contacted me to see if I was still interested.

When the time came to change I didn't feel like talking Jaguars into selling me a car, so I bought a MPW Silver Shadow. This was a nice car, but I missed my Jaguar and when due for another change went back to them. By this time Lex sales personnel had been changed and the Jaguar man was Keith Hopkins, an old friend, so I bought another new XJ6 from him.

In November 1977 the factory announced that production of the coupé had ceased. Still hankering after one I rang my pal to see if he had any left. He had two, one in my favourite colour of dark blue, so I did a deal. It is a very sad but well-known fact that Jaguar quality had been deteriorating

For me the Daimler 250 never reached the same position in my affections as its 6-cylinder brethren. This specimen was the pride and joy of my next door neighbour who sadly suffered a stroke which prevented him from driving. So saddened did he become by the sight of it in his garage that his wife asked me to buy it. I kept it for some time but never really liked it.

for some years. I noticed it on customers' cars and every car I bought was worse than its predecessor. The coupé was an absolute disgrace. Efforts to have it put right under warranty didn't meet with much success, so I had it gone over in my own workshops, my own coachbuilders and, of course, at my own expense. It took about three months and quite a lot of money to get it in the condition it should have been in when I bought it.

I wonder how many people realise how near we were to losing this grand British car through sheer bad quality control, lack of pride in the job and a management who didn't care. I wonder, too, if Jaguar Cars realise how much they owe to people like me (and there are thousands of us) who loyally continued to purchase their cars in spite of the way they were turned out.

Fortunately, the present administration are on the right lines and all the later Series 3 car I get in are first class. In fact, having driven everything, I would say the present 5.3 saloon is one of the best cars in the world.

I still have the coupé; it is my favourite and after nine years has only covered 9,400 miles, has only been out in the rain about half a dozen times and is like new.

In mid 1978 I got bitten by the E-Type bug. A customer bought a V12 roadster and brought it in to be sorted out. I gave it a long road test and realised I had forgotten what a nice car it was. Reckoning I could just about afford one with the help of the traditional friendly Bank Manager, I looked around.

An advert in Motor Sport attracted me for a V12 roadster in primrose. It was only at Chessington so I went to see it. To my surprise I found the garage was owned by James Tilling, an old friend from the racing days, so

My first E-Type MGF 113L, was finished in Primrose with black hard top. I had forgotten how wonderful these cars are until I recently drove a customer's example.

we got together. The car had done a big mileage, but had done it well. The body was in very sound condition, it went well, so I bought it.

Stephen and I had a lot of fun with it, and then one day I saw an advert in 'Exchange & Mart'. It was for a V12 roadster in signal red, all the usual bits and pieces and a genuine 29,000 miles. What's more it was a local number. Very intrigued, as I had not seen the car around, I rang up. It turned out the car was in Guildford, not very far away, so I went to see it. It was extremely nice so, after a bit of hassle when the vendor tried to gazump me, I bought it and sold the yellow one. I still have this car which has done only 33,000 miles even now and thoroughly enjoy it.

By now the XJS had been around a bit. I had driven a few and thought they were grand. One weekend, looking through the advertisements in the *The Sunday Times*, I spotted a likely looking specimen at Stratstone's which was reasonably priced. Next day I rang up Roy Keyes, an old friend of mine who was a Director of Stratstone, and asked him what it was like. He said, "Why don't you borrow it for a week and find out?" Within half an hour my driver was on the train to get it. I had a smashing week and at the end of it there was no way I was going to hand it back, so an XJS joined the Jaguar stable. It gave me a lot of pleasure for about eighteen months, but by this time Stephen's Jensen consisted of more Isopon than metal and his feet were in danger of going through the floor, so he bought the XJS. He still has it, so it is sort of still in the family and I drive it often.

I really think these cars are fabulous. Why people spend more than twice as much on exotic continental GTs when the XJS gives the same performance in more comfort I will never know. This may sound strange coming from someone who has just finished singing the praises of the Facel Vega and

The XJS is surely the last word in fast, silent and comfortable travel. I sold my own specimen here to Stephen after many happy miles of ownership. Stephen has had the good sense to hang on to it.

Iso Grifo, but of course that was 25 years ago and the pattern of motoring has changed considerably in that time. For present day road conditions I feel the XJS cannot be bettered.

Shortly afterwards I was tempted again. An acquaintance approached me to ask if I would be interested in an XJ6 belonging to a friend of his. It belonged to a widow and had been her husband's car. More out of politeness than interest I went to see it and found one of the last Series 2 saloons with only 7,000 miles on the clock. Mechanically and inside it was like new but the body showed signs of the poor original finish and had a few minor battle scars.

It was nothing that couldn't be put right, so I bought it. There were six months tax and MOT left, so for six months I enjoyed the convenience of four door Jaguar motoring and then sold it.

I purchased my 20th Jaguar last year. Circumstances arose whereby I needed a four door car again for a few weeks. As some long runs were involved it had to be another XJ6 so I looked around and finished up with a silver Series 3 4.2. It is such a nice car that I have kept it, using it most of the time to keep the mileage down on the coupé.

Since commencing this chapter the new XJ40 has been announced and through the kindness of Keith Hopkins of Lex (now re-named Weybridge Automobiles, to distinguish it from the less illustrious Austin-Rover side of the business) I have been able to try both the 2.9 and 3.6 versions.

It must have been an extremely difficult task to improve on the Series 3 XJ6 without going into the Rolls Royce price bracket, but it has been done. It is true the 3.6 Sovereign version costs more than the Series 3 but not in relation to what you get for your money. Externally there is not very much difference, especially the XJ6 model which retains the twin headlamps, but mechanically it is all new. The new engine is superb. I had been told it was rough compared with the old 4.2 unit but the two examples I drove showed no sign of roughness at any speed. Suspension on the old car was so good it is not easy to detect any improvement on a short run without

This is one of the very last of the Series Two saloons which I bought because it seemed to me such a perfect specimen that I couldn't refuse it. Like so many of the fine cars in my life however it passed on in due course.

Above left: *I kept my second E-type much longer than the first. It was a magnificent specimen in Signal Red with that wonderful V12 engine; as different from a Ferrari as beer from Chianti but just as enjoyable.*

Above: *I used the E-type for many events and here it is at a JDC Rally. When the weather is good such events are the greatest of fun and we were lucky on this occasion.*

Left: *Another view of the gaggle of E-types at the same JDC Rally.*

passengers, but no doubt when fully loaded the self levelling effect of the new system is a distinct advantage. Brakes and steering are up to the expected Jaguar standards and moving the rear brakes outboard is a long overdue modification from a servicing point of view. Interior appointments reach a new level of luxury in the Sovereign, even more so I believe in the Daimler version, but I have yet to see one of these.

My last XJ6 was a 4.2 Series 3 car. This model is a truly great performer with a standard of comfort and silence not equalled even by "The Best Car in The World"; judged by any test you may care to apply.

I drove the 3.6 Sovereign first, which was probably a mistake as, by comparison, the 2.9 XJ6 seemed a little tame. Looking at it in its own right as a luxury car costing under £17,000, it must surely knock spots off the opposition. The Sovereign can only be described as magnificent. The new all-alloy 24 valve engine gives it performance and flexibility superior to any of its competitors that I have driven. In fact, I cannot see that it has any competition. The new ZF 4-speed automatic transmission is faultless in operation and the whole car must surely be the ultimate in silent, effortless motoring. I am very grateful to Keith for giving me the opportunity to bring my Jaguar story up to date and will try even harder with my football pools coupon from now on!

Jaguars have undoubtedly played a large part in my motoring career as, apart from my own cars, I must have driven literally hundreds of them. I have driven examples of every model made except the first SSI and the D Type. Much to my regret the D-Type always evaded me when they were more or less current models and I feel it extremely unlikely I will ever drive one now. Genuine cars are worth a fortune these days. I wouldn't dare ask if I could borrow one and I would get no satisfaction from driving a modern reproduction however good it might be,

When I first became interested in them they were looked down upon by

A fitting tailpiece to my account of Jaguar motoring is provided by a last shot of my first Jaguar parked with Hilda's little A30; representing two extremes of performance at the time when the British motor industry was a force to be reckoned with.

the pundits. It seemed like pure snobbery to me; the Bentley, Alvis, Lagonda brigade resented the fact that humbler mortals could now buy a car that looked and performed like theirs for a quarter of the price. Now they are considered to be one of Britain's prestige cars, used by the Queen Mother and other members of the Royal Family, the Prime Minister and every local Mayor who can talk his long suffering ratepayers into paying for one. I won't mention Arthur Scargill. You can't win 'em all!

9
A BENTLEY SAGA

Bentleys have played a modest part in my motoring career in recent years and my association with them goes back further than that. To most dedicated motorists of my generation they represent the golden age – large powerful open cars (didn't it ever rain then?), burbling exhausts and the freedom of the open road. My interest in them began when I was a schoolboy. There were a few in the district and I could recognise the distinctive exhaust note from a long way off and would stop whatever I was doing until I had seen it go by. Moreover, on my frequent and usually highly illicit visits to Brooklands I watched people like Birkin, Davis, Barnato, Kidston, Benjafield and all the other 'Bentley Boys' sweeping round the track, high up on the banking, carrying all before them. Through the motoring press I was able to follow their exploits at Le Mans and other important races.

What true Englishman could fail to feel a stirring of the blood at the sight of this magnificent line up of Bentleys, some "real" and some "special" on the Brooklands banking, the frosty concrete revealing the pattern of tyre treads made as they took station. Soon the low temperature will be forgotten as enthusiasts compare notes and the memories of years gone by are recalled and savoured . . .

We seldom saw one at the garage when I was an apprentice. Occasionally a local owner might bring one in for something minor like cleaning the plugs, but for anything major they would go to the London Service Dept. We never had them in for resale either. As mentioned earlier, the MD was a well-built, middle-aged gent who preferred the comfort and top gear performance of the big Yanks. Even after all these years I find the thought of old 'Stodge' rowing a vintage Bentley along highly amusing. As a result I was about seventeen when I drove my first Bentley, a $6\frac{1}{2}$ litre. It was only round the block and I got the drive through pure cheek. A local chauffeur had two cars in his charge, a straight eight Studebaker and a Morris Major. He used to bring both of them in for maintenance. He was a friendly type and I got to know him quite well. One day he arrived with this 6½-litre Bentley which had apparently replaced the Studebaker.

It was the first 6-cylinder Bentley I had seen at close quarters and what a magnificent sight it was. We all stood around admiring it and in the course of conversation he mentioned that it had a starting handle which was quite useless as no-one could possibly swing it. I was quite strong as a lad and, anyway, swinging engines was more of a knack than anything else so I bet him I could. He thought this quite funny and said if I could do it he would let me drive the car round the block. Much to his surprise, having got it over the first compression, I swung it easily. To his credit he kept his word. Looking back I feel it was a jolly decent thing to do. It was an extremely large and powerful car; I was just a young lad and had only held a driving licence for a few months. Had I pranged it he would almost certainly have got the sack.

In my collection of model cars is a miniature of the Bentley 3-litre exactly like this charming example of a "real" Bentley photographed at a BDC gathering. Wonderful as the 4½, Speed 6 and 8-litre Bentleys are, the original little 3-litres have a unique, almost Edwardian charm all of their own, and I prefer them.

After this I did manage to get my hands on the odd 3-litre but it was not until much later and the arrival of the Rolls-built 3½-litre that I drove them in any numbers. This was entirely due to the Film Studios next door. Many of the more affluent stars and producers had them and used to leave them with us for attention during the day. There were all sorts of body styles, most of them very beautiful. The cars themselves varied. Some of the owners were keen motorists, taking a pride in their car and their driving. Regrettably, others just had them because it was the car to be seen in. They didn't appreciate the superb engineering and most of them couldn't have driven the wind out of a paper bag. I'm sure the cars knew and, within a mile of driving one, I could tell what the owner was like. When the 4¼-litre came out one or two of the keener types made the change. There was very little difference in performance; maximum speed was about the same but acceleration in top gear was improved and it seemed less fussy at high revs.

I did not drive an MX overdrive model until after the war.

At one time in the early thirties we had a well connected salesman who

My second Bentley was this 1935 3½-litre Mulliner saloon photographed as a back drop to Hilda at Claremont Lake, Esher. Built only four years after the Rolls Royce takeover this Derby-chassis car represented the best of both worlds in the Bentley/Rolls-Royce marriage and had great character. Sadly I found it rather heavy to drive in modern traffic conditions which are much more demanding than they were when the car was new 50 years ago. I felt obliged to sell it when I broke my leg.

announced one day that he was borrowing a Bentley from a London trader to show to a client, and he duly arrived in the ex-Barnato Blue Train Speed Six. Typically of him, instead of reversing into the showroom and lining it up with the others, he drove straight in and left it in the middle of the floor. The Sales Manager went mad so I got it, reversed it out, turned around and reversed back in again. It was an incident of no significance at the time but, of course, in recent years that car has become a legend, reaching its pinnacle last year when it was sold for nearly a quarter of a million pounds. I have a beautiful Western model of it in my collection and when I show it to anyone, or if the car is being discussed, I say with exaggerated nonchalance, "I drove that car before the war".

In late 1946, when I joined HWM, we were busy making cars roadworthy that had been stored during the war. Amongst these was a 3½-litre Mulliner-bodied Bentley belonging to the local MP. He wanted it in 100% condition so it was agreed that, after we had got it going, I would use it for a few weeks to sort out any problems. So I had my own personal Bentley. At that time I was courting a girl from Iver, Bucks, and our favourite pub was the Two Brewers at Henley. I can still remember those fast runs down the almost deserted Bath Road. Being a close coupled sports saloon there was very little room in the back, but then you can't have everything!

Soon after we resumed normal business we became friendly with Hugh Hunter, a pre-war racing and rally driver, famed for his performance in a challenge race at Brooklands for the fastest sports car.

He had several cars, including one or two veterans, but for personal transport he had a 4¼-litre Vanden Plas two door saloon. It was a beautiful car and is illustrated at the bottom of page 199 in Johnnie Green's book. I believe, but cannot be certain now, that he drove this car in a pre-war

The 3½-litre at Kensington Gardens again surrounded by other delectable machinery of its period. I find Bentleys of any year highly desirable and although they are so very different in character over the years they all maintain that unique feeling of mechanical quality confined to Bentley and Rolls Royce alone.

Monte Carlo Rally. He lived at Esher, quite handy for us, and we looked after the Bentley. It was without doubt the nicest $4\frac{1}{4}$ I have driven. I remember that he once lost the securing catch for one of the swivelling quarter lights in the doors and it was impossible to replace it. He was a perfectionist and this upset him. I understood this. It would have annoyed me too, so I made him a new one by hand from a small block of dural. It took hours of delicate filing but when finished and highly polished, it was difficult to tell it from the other one. I hadn't told him what I was doing in case I made a mess of it, so he was both surprised and delighted when I put it on.

The next Bentley I used was far more interesting. John Heath had a friend with a vintage $4\frac{1}{2}$-litre open 4 seater. He went abroad for two or three months, left the car with us and asked John to use it regularly to keep the wheels turning. Strangely enough, neither Heath or Abecassis liked vintage cars although both were very keen drivers. I asked John once why and he replied, "Why be bloody uncomfortable if you haven't got to?" There was a certain logic in this but I didn't mind being uncomfortable so when he asked me to drive it I could not get in quickly enough.

This car was the real thing – sketchy wings, big tank, aero screens, etc., and in perfect mechanical order. Once the rather tricky gearbox was mastered it was sheer joy to drive and I went everywhere in it.

It was reputed to be a Team car but I took this with a pinch of salt as almost any open $4\frac{1}{2}$ is 'an ex-Team car'. Years later, in one of my Bentley books, there was a list of team cars with their registration numbers. One

This most beautiful Derby Bentley photographed at Brooklands is owned by Johnnie Green, Author of "Fifty Years of the Marque", one of the Bentley "Bibles". To my eye this is one of the most perfectly formed examples of the coachbuilder's art from the inter-war years.

of them looked familiar so I turned up my photo album and there it was. So I have driven one of the team cars.

The next one was a 3-litre. We had a customer, Mr Ronald Quilter, who owned a Big Six Citroën. He rang me one day saying he had owned an open 3-litre Bentley when he was young and wanted his son to have one when he left University. Would I find him one? A chap I knew from the racing days dabbled in vintage Bentleys so I went over to his place near Aylesbury to see what he had. Just inside the door was the very thing, a boat tail two seater with a little dickey seat in the tail. It was painted grey with dark green wings and wheels and looked very smart. It went as well as it looked so I bought it. I rang Quilter who sent me a cheque and said as his son wouldn't want it for a couple of months, would I use it and get out all the bugs? So once more I had my own Bentley. I used it a lot, including a trip to Goodwood on a freezing cold day that later turned to rain. I had the most miserable run home, wet, cold, the wipers quite inadequate and a nagging feeling that perhaps John Heath had a point!

This was the end of my Bentley motoring at other people's expense apart from test runs, demonstration runs, etc., on the Mk VI, R Type and S Type. I wasn't too struck on these at the time but have got to like them since. Apart from the fact that one's driving style alters with advancing years, there is no doubt that the modern Bentley is more suited to present day traffic conditions.

My house is on a corner and about 20 years ago I became aware of an old boy occasionally coming along the side road in a Mk VI Bentley. I used to wave and say "good morning" when he walked past with his dog, but never got to know him. One Saturday morning his next door neighbour, who was a customer of mine, told me he was selling it on doctor's orders. I told him I was interested, but he said I had better hurry as it was almost sold. I went straight round there and it was true enough – two people had looked at it and were coming back later. I was shaken when he told me

My first Bentley was this 1950 Mk.6 Standard Steel saloon. It was purchased under rather odd circumstances and owned by me for many years. I used the Bentley for a wide variety of functions both locally near Walton and in the Isle of Wight and won many prizes with it. Eventually I sold it to my good friend Dr. Bennett who had coveted it for years. He still owns and maintains it beautifully having a love of Bentleys only equalled by his dedication as a Doctor.

his asking price. Incredible as it may seem, being in the motor trade, I am fundamentally honest, so felt morally bound to tell him it was worth more than that. He was quite taken aback as apparently the other two wanted to chip him fifty quid, but he was a gentleman and said that as I had been honest with him I could still have it for the asking price if I could produce the money before they came back.

There was no time to lose so I went home, turned out my wallet, Hilda's handbag, slit the mattress open, took up the floorboards, robbed the television fund and the dog's vet bill fund, went round to the garage and emptied the till. That was not quite enough so I borrowed the rest. I put it all in a plastic bag, went back and found the other characters had not yet arrived. We tipped it all out on the kitchen table, he counted it and I had my first Bentley.

I kept it for years, improving it all the time. I took it to numerous classic car meetings, pageants, etc. It went to the Isle of Wight and carried the Carnival Queen on a parade. It was in our local parade for the Queen's Silver Jubilee, two of my neighbours' daughters went to their weddings in it and it was the conveyance for Robin and Batman in a local charity fair for needy children. I was very fond of that car and drove it a lot. It never failed to start however long I left it unused and never let me down. I fully intended to keep it until, like its previous owner, I became too old to drive it, but fate had other ideas.

One day I visited an old friend with a Renault agency in Weybridge and there in his showroom, amongst all the tin boxes, was a gleaming black 3½-litre pre-war Bentley saloon. He told me he had bought it for his father to tinker with to give him an interest. It was not quite finished but the old man had got fed up with it. In no time at all we had agreed a price. A

Here is the Mk.6 pausing outside my garage in the Isle of Wight having just won another first prize in a local Concours.

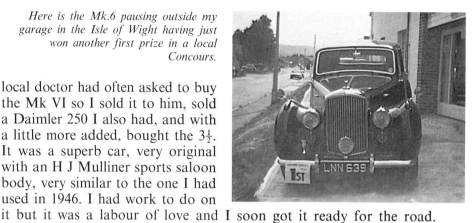

local doctor had often asked to buy the Mk VI so I sold it to him, sold a Daimler 250 I also had, and with a little more added, bought the 3½. It was a superb car, very original with an H J Mulliner sports saloon body, very similar to the one I had used in 1946. I had work to do on it but it was a labour of love and I soon got it ready for the road.

I found the steering very heavy for normal use. Once rolling it wasn't too bad but it became much more of a special occasion car than the Mk VI had been. I enjoyed it though, took it to various shows and BDC meetings, a charity fete in the Isle of Wight and one or two local functions. Just to sit behind that long bonnet and those two gorgeous P100 headlamps was ample compensation for the heavy controls.

One winter morning I was clumsy enough to slip on an icy path and break

Hidden away in the midst of this gaggle of cars at a Bentley Drivers Club meeting in Kensington Gardens is my faithful Mk.6 The later Crewe-built Bentleys are lined up to face their Cricklewood-born ancestors; providing a central promenade for the onlookers.

my left leg. It was a complicated fracture and other problems ensued which I won't go into here. Suffice it to say that it was three months before I could drive and even then could not manage the Bentley. I had got friendly with Mike Walker, a Rolls and Bentley specialist in Woking and he offered to buy it so, reluctantly, I let him have it.

I could not get the Bentley bug out of my system so decided to buy one with automatic transmission. The earliest automatic Bentley is the R Type so that's what it had to be.

Literally buried under bunting and boarding, the faithful Mk.6, my original Bentley love, wins yet another prize at a meeting in the Isle of Wight.

I found one in good general condition but the lower half needed painting. I had this done and, during the summer, did the rounds again. I sold it then for two reasons. For one thing the lock up garage I kept it in was difficult to get into with a big car, necessitating many backward and forward movements. The steering, although much lighter than the $3\frac{1}{2}$, was still too heavy for me. By the time it was safely inside I was shagged out. Secondly, the lower half painting had been poorly done and I had several adverse comments at the various shows. Most classic car owners attend these meetings not only for the pleasure of seeing other nice cars but to show off their own. Pride of possession is all part of the fun. I couldn't feel proud of my R-Type so it lost its purpose.

It seemed power steering would have to be a feature of my next Bentley so that meant an S-Type. I bought a 1957 model from a BDC member. It solved all the problems and, in spite of the additional length, was no trouble to put away. It was a nice car but didn't have much poke so when I was offered a price which showed me a small profit I sold it. I then looked around for a 1959 model as these had an 8 to 1 compression ratio giving them much better performance. Through an advert in *Motor Sport* I located one near Royston and Stephen and I went up in the E-Type to see it. Like every other car I've been to see it did not match up to the owner's lyrical description, but it was a good sound car so I bought it. Little effort and not too much expense was needed to make it pristine and once more I had a Bentley I could be proud of. Over the next $2\frac{1}{2}$ years I took it to various functions including two BDC Silverstone race meetings and their Kensington Gardens concours. Although not like the older Bentleys, it was a nice car to drive and I became quite fond of it.

However, early in the year the owner of my rented lock up told me he might be moving and that, if he did, I would lose the use of the garage. This was a blow; it would have been almost impossible to find another one long enough to take an S-Type. I was wondering what to do about it when I was approached by a trader friend of mine who wanted to buy the car for an American customer of his. His offer was so good that, on the basis that it was better to sell it now for a good price than have to sell it in a hurry for what I could get later on, I let him have it.

I moved forward 20 years in time when I bought my third Bentley, this 1954 R-Type purchased in order to provide me with an automatic transmission to get me through a period of weakness in my broken leg. I chose this model because it was the earliest of the Type fitted with labour saving transmission and thoroughly enjoyed it; parting with it as usual regretfully.

I had no choice in replacing it; the only Bentley that would go in my own garage was a T-Type. I wasn't keen on them but decided it was better than not having one at all. I wanted a 1969 model as these had many mechanical improvements over the earlier cars, including a better gearbox. At the same time they retained most of the old features like solid wheel trims, picnic tables and a less ornate cockpit. I found one through an advertisement, a one-owner car in my favourite midnight blue. Much to my surprise I got to like it. It is true it wasn't a 'proper' Bentley but at least

To my mind the last of the "classic" Bentleys (if not the last of the "real" Bentleys – that was in about 1930) was the 1959 "S" Type. Like all Bentleys of my experience this was a delightful car and sold with reluctance.

Above: *Much to my regret the previous owner of my "S" Type insisted on keeping his original number plate and I was obliged by Swansea to fit this 1964 plate. Eventually I was able to bring things back to normal by buying another car to provide a suffix-free registration number so that I could motor with my mind at rest.*

Above right: *Here is the "S" Type with its proper number at Kensington in the following year. I always felt the 6 cylinder "S" Type to be a much nicer car than the V8 and somehow when driving it one was never conscious of its truly great size.*

Below: *The last Bentley that I owned was this beautiful 1969 T-Type and it was a much nicer car than I had expected it to be. Somehow it seemed more stable than the Shadow equivalent but I may have allowed myself to have been charmed by the radiator. I sold it when I disposed of my garage as it became difficult to maintain in the manner to which it had become accustomed.*

it had a decent radiator, not that old flat thing.

I sold it when I retired last year as, without proper workshop facilities, there were very few servicing jobs I could do myself. This also applies to my Jaguar to a certain extent but at least I have good Jaguar connections and wouldn't get quite such a striping if I was forced to have something done.

I may one day get another Mk VI. I feel they give modern comforts with vintage characteristics. What I would really like is an open Speed Six, but Hilda won't let me sell the house.

Some women never get their priorities right!

10
THE LAST TWENTY YEARS

When I left HWM to start my own business I was virtually turning the clock back twenty years. For one thing the garage was on the site of the original HW Motors premises and for another I was back to working on cars during the day, doing the paper work in the evenings and operating the petrol pumps at weekends. It was a bit of a challenge but I enjoyed it. For a start I was my own boss. I suppose in a way I had been before; George Abecassis was very decent in that respect, letting me do pretty much as I liked. For my part I was loyal to him, did not take advantage and always did my best for the Company. Nevertheless this was different. Whether I had butter on my bread, margarine or nothing at all depended on my own efforts. This being so I got stuck in, because I like butter on my bread!

I suppose the thing I missed at first was the glamour and prestige of being a Director of a nationally known company dealing in exotic motor cars. I missed the cars themselves and the trips abroad. This soon passed. I got one or two Astons in, a couple of Facel HK500s and continued to service Ringo Starr's Facel 2. The continental trips had dried up anyway with the demise of Facel and Iso, so I was no worse off there.

A view of the "right crowd" failing to crowd the Test Hill at Brooklands after restitution by the hard working Brooklands Society. These gatherings at the cradle of British motor sport arouse memories in the minds of those of us old enough to have been there in its heyday and thoughts of "what might have been" in the younger generation.

With one full time bod and a shower of part-timers we began to make progress and before long I was looking around for more staff. Within a couple of weeks I was joined by Colin Westbury. Colin had come to me at HWM in the early fifties and, apart from a break to do his National Service, had been with me ever since. He is still with me, a Director of my little Company and in charge of our garage on the Isle of Wight.

Before long I was to have my last trip to Paris for Facel spares. Some years previously I had sold an automatic HK500 to a friend in Scotland, Tom Carruthers. I had only been at the garage a few months when he telephoned to say his gearbox had packed up. His local garage had it but could get no parts. I knew that if HWM hadn't got them there were none in the UK, but Facel were still operating a Spares Dept at Puteaux, so I gave them a ring. Tom had given me a list of parts required, Facel had some of them but not all, so I then rang Chryslers in Antwerp. By good fortune they had the rest. I had bought a Mini for local running around, so on the grounds of economy, decided to use it for the job.

Catching an early flight from Lydd to Ostend, I was in Antwerp by lunchtime, picked up the parts and set off for Paris. Arriving in Ghent about six o'clock I reckoned I had done enough for one day and put up for the night in a charming little hotel facing the town square. Next morning I continued via Lille and Arras to Paris. Facel still had all the old staff and they greeted me like a long lost brother and it was great fun. I left next morning and got home in time to despatch the parts to Tom. It was a fair old three days trip in a Mini but I enjoyed it.

My own car at this time was a Humber Super Snipe which was a bit woolly but comfortable, nice inside and had a fair turn of speed. I was quite happy with it until one of my customers with a particularly nice Jaguar was given a company car. The Jaguar was put up for sale and I couldn't resist it. The business did well. Most of the cars we serviced were fairly ordinary, but with lots of Jaguars, several Astons, one Ferrari, two Facels, several Jensens and a Bentley on the books, we usually had a certain amount of class about the place.

My old pal Dick Williams had left Mumbles and taken a pub in Sevenoaks, so he was near enough for us to look after his Aston drop head. A friend of mine who had a car showroom but no workshop gave us his repair work. He dealt in good class cars, including Rolls and Bentley, and I remember a Buick Riviera that gave us a lot of trouble with oil pressure problems.

My two partners lived in Dumfries. They were brothers and, although elderly, enjoyed fast cars. One of them had purchased two Facels from me, an HK500 and our first Facel 2 with a manual gearbox. He had ordered another one with the 6.7 litre engine but they went out of production before he could get it. Not being able to make up his mind what to buy instead, he purchased a 4.2 E-Type Jaguar as a stop gap. He liked it so much he kept it and had several more, including two V12s. I supplied some of them and always enjoyed the delivery journey. He also had a small car and, just before I left HWM, he bought a 1275cc Mini Cooper S. He found this great fun and purchased another one from me. Before taking up to him we fitted high compression pistons and tweaked it a bit. I didn't get a chance to drive it after it was run in but he told me it went like a scalded cat. This car had two petrol tanks. They were connected and could both be refilled from one orifice, although two were fitted. At running in speeds I was over the Scotch border before needing petrol. I pulled into a small garage and asked for 12 gallons. "It won't hold 12 gallons", said the attendant. He was very sure of himself and appeared to think I was a typical Southerner trying to take the mickey out of a poor Scotsman. I let him rabbit on for a bit and then pointed out the second tank. That shut him up, but it was with considerable ill grace that he gave me my 12 gallons.

For some years I continued to make regular journeys to Dumfries in my Jaguar, although not always the same one as I changed them frequently. It was always a pleasant trip. I would stay the night at the Cairndale, a first class hotel and we would have a jolly good meal and a chat about the business. Next morning I would leave for home, stopping off at Penrith to see Hilda's sister.

The distance between us caused a few problems at times, so once we were well established my Scots friends baled out and Stephen became my partner. He still is and, strange to relate, we are still friends. We had a customer with a weekend cottage in the Isle of Wight. He knew Hilda and I had spent several holidays there and that we were fond of it. One day he asked me if I wanted to buy a garage there. My first reaction was to say no, but two of my chaps overhead the conversation. Next thing I knew I had Colin and the other two pleading with me to buy it and send them out there. I agreed to go over to see it. It was an attractive place and situated where I thought we could make a living so, after several visits by Stephen and myself, we took the plunge. Colin is still there, a typical Islander by now and Chairman of the Vectis Historic Vehicle Club.

Hilda had a succession of BMC 1100s but one day we saw a Fiat 850 Sports Coupé parked by the road. It was a pretty little car and she was quite taken by it. I ordered one from the local Fiat dealer. There was a waiting time of two months but eventually it came along. The rubber mats spoilt it so I took it up to Wood and Pickett where my old pal Joe Knott had a set of pile carpets made. It turned out to be the worst car I have ever bought and put me off Fiats for life. As soon as it was expedient we changed it for a new Riley Kestrel.

Towards the end of 1974 an Insurance Assessor came to look at a damaged vehicle. Having known each other many years, he knew my background and asked if I wanted to buy a Facel Vega. I was a bit interested so he told me it was an HK500 gathering dust in a coachbuilders at Hayes, which was not too far away, so I went to see it. I recognised the car as one sold through

Opposite top: *The running boards on the MG Y-Type saloon confuse most onlookers into imagining it to be a pre-war car. Its character, real vintage interior and general feeling of quality overcome the incredible lack of performance.*

Opposite bottom: *Another view of the Y-Type with first prize at an Isle of Wight meeting. These classic little saloons sold well for a short time after the war before the new wave of modern shapes such as the Morris Minor and new Hillman Minx rendered them sadly outdated.*

Charles Follett to the Marchioness of Huntley. It was tatty but sound so I bought it. It needed considerable work. We hadn't the space at Walton for long term projects so, having got it running, I took it to the Island.

It was right up Colin's street. Having been with me at HWM he knew the cars and it was just the sort of job he liked. The chassis was completely overhauled. a local coachbuilder did the body and the whole thing took about eighteen months though it seemed more like eighteen years. I solved the spares problem by buying a very down-and-out one for a small sum and dismantling it. We had a lot of fun with that car. A Facel Vega Owners' Club had been formed. I was made President and we went to classic car meetings all over the country. When I wasn't using it over here it lived on the Island, becoming well known at the various shows, carnivals and fetes. I kept it for about eight years. It gave no trouble and was eventually sold to a German who took it back to Munich.

The classic car bug tends to get a hold of you once it has taken the first bite, so when I saw a 1935 Oldsmobile advertised at a reasonable price in Cobham I went to investigate. It was in pretty good condition, wanted painting but there was very little rust and it was a runner. I soon found the brakes were almost non-existent and I discovered the wipers didn't work when it started to drizzle. Although the journey was only five miles, it was misery and I was thankful to arrive home without hitting anything.

They were still working on the Facel in the Isle of Wight so, not wishing to overload them with non-profitable work, I had the Oldsmobile painted and re-chromed over here and put some brakes on it. By that time Colin

My 1935 Oldsmobile provided much enjoyable motoring and had many of the qualities of the best European cars at a fraction of the cost. It would cruise effortlessly and quietly all day and although its roadholding was none too great, was a sedate and comfortable means of transport. This shot was taken outside my Walton-on-Thames garage and used by the Surrey Herald *to illustrate an article about me and my cars.*

had finished the mechanical work on the Facel and it was in the coachbuilders, so I took the Oldsmobile across for finishing. Apart from a trip over here for one of the Seven Springs Pageants and another one for our local Jubilee Parade, it has lived on the Island ever since.

During the summer there are carnivals every weekend at the Island's seaside towns and there is always a parade. Frequently the Oldsmobile carries the Carnival Queen (I'm never invited on these occasions, Colin hogs that one for himself) and sometimes it is transport for the local dignitaries. In addition to the carnivals there are several classic car shows and charity functions and we are usually amongst the prizewinners. The car is now so much a part of the Island that I would probably be lynched in Newport's town square if I ever sold it.

The Oldsmobile drives away from another event in which it came first in class.

On one visit to the Island I was told about an antique dealer who had bought all the effects of a recently deceased local lady, including a pre-war Morris 8. Thinking it worth investigating I went to see him. The car was only just pre-war, a late 1939 4 door Series E, in generally sound condition and with obvious possibilities. After the usual haggling I bought it, we did the little mechanical work necessary to bring it up to scratch, had it recellulosed in the original black finish and kept it for some time. One day I was told of a Bull Nose Morris Cowley standing at the side of a house in a small village. It was well inland and away from the normal tourist traffic so I felt there may be something in it. Sure enough, almost hidden by long grass and thistles was an open 4 seater with the hood up but no side screens in place.

It was an absolute tragedy. The car had obviously been in tip top condition when left there and was just beginning to deteriorate. I called at the house and an elderly lady told me the car was her husband's who was the local clockmaker with a workshop behind the church. With some difficulty I found it and the old chap asked me in, sitting me on a rough hand made stool. He was a wonderful man and his little workshop was full of old clocks, watches, bulb horns, acetylene lamps, some in working order and some obviously not. He knew the history of them all and took delight in fetching out more things from under piles of rubbish, talking about them all the time. With some difficulty I got him round to the Morris Cowley. Yes it was his, he had owned it for many years. Some years previously it had been completely renovated for him with a real paint and varnish job, none of your new-fangled cellulose, and it hadn't been used since. He thought he might sell it one day but not to me. The car had been supplied new by the local Morris agent in 1925 and had never been off the island. He would only sell it to another Islander who would have to promise not to take it to the mainland. I didn't press him. His pride in the Isle of Wight and its heritage was plain to see and I admired him for it. He showed me some more of his treasures but eventually I had to go. It was a most delightful look into the past. I have no idea whether he, the car, or his Aladdin's cave are still there, I hope so. I expect the locals know all about him but there is no way his exact locality will ever by revealed by me.

One day Dick Williams rang to say he had sold his Aston DB Mk 3 drop-head and bought a DB4 GT and would I collect it for a service and check over. I was pretty chuffed about this. The GT with its more powerful twin plug engine and short wheelbase was about the most desirable of Astons. It was a long time since I had driven one and I looked forward to collecting it from Sevenoaks. Dick kept it for some time and over the years it gave a fair bit of trouble which was not always easy to rectify. Some of the parts were the same as the standard DB4 and DB5, but a lot of things were special to the GT and spares became a problem. Most of them were in the hands of specialists who were, understandably, reluctant to part with them. At one stage it went through a period of rough running. It seemed like carburation, but not much goes wrong with Webers and the float levels were correct and the jets hadn't been altered. Suspecting an air leak we removed the carburettors, but there was nothing apparently wrong with the gaskets. I took the car over to an old friend, Alan Southern, who had a racing and tuning establishment at Hartley Wintney. He was the best man on Webers you could hope to find, but a morning with him didn't get us anywhere. In the end I took the carburettors off again, stripped them out, rebuilt them and fitted new flange gaskets. The trouble was cured but it was a mystery as there was no obvious reason for it. Poor Alan is no longer with us. He was a dedicated man and would work day and night to finish a job he had promised. I'm sure it killed him in the end.

Not long after this the Aston suffered a burnt piston. It was one of the two fed by the suspect carburettor and I'm certain it was caused by weak mixture. The only other reason could have been plugs but, although I had experimented with different plugs when trying to cure the rough running, they all had a suitable heat range. Unfortunately, the high compression GT pistons were unobtainable so I had to fit standard DB4 items. It lost a fair bit of poke through this but it was more tractable. Eventually Dick had trouble with his left leg and changed the GT for an automatic DB6. I knew the feeling, having been forced to do the same with my Bentley. I like automatics. With the exception of the E-Type, all my Jaguars have been so equipped for the last eighteen years, but some cars seem as though they should have a gearbox and I think the Aston is one of them.

In the early seventies I had a certain amount of involvement with Opels. I felt I was getting into a rut with my Jaguars, but there was nothing else that appealed to me until the new shape Opel Commodore was announced.

Three contemporary classics from my collection seen at another Isle of Wight Charity Show. The Oldsmobile was somewhat unusual in such gatherings and nearly always won a prize. It did so on this occasion, rather showing up my 3½ and the HK500 entered with it.

It looked a nice car so I went over to Driftbridge Garage at Epsom and tried their demonstrator. As a result I ordered a GS Coupé. There was a few weeks delay for the GS model so, as I had a punter for my XJ6, I bought a Manta as an interim car. I was impressed with the Manta when it was first exhibited at Earls Court. One of my customers had purchased one. He was delighted with it and on the odd occasions I had driven it I liked it too. His was the 1600cc model but Driftbridge had an 1800, finished in pale yellow with black vinyl top and it looked a picture. We liked this car so much that when Hilda was due for another car I bought her a Manta Berlinetta.

Eventually the Commodore came along and it was an extremely nice car. The GS had twin carburettors which gave it plenty of poke and the steering, brakes and road holding were first class. When it was still only a few weeks old Hilda and I were driving through Hounslow. It was raining hard and there were frequent heavy gusts of wind. Two chaps were unloading a furniture van when suddenly a big gust of wind lifted one of the big rear doors off its hinges and it sailed through the air and crashed, edge on, into my near side door, just below the window. It made a large vee in the panel, but had it been a few inches higher Hilda might well have been killed.

My coachbuilder, working under the threat of terrible consequences if the job wasn't right, made a really good job of it and you couldn't see it had ever been damaged.

Soon after I got it back I had to go to Bexhill. Passing through Herstmonceux, I caught up with a tractor towing a trailer. When just clear of the village, he took a wide sweep to turn into a gateway so I stopped. Round a bend facing me came a Bedford van going at a fair old lick and it had to pull up sharply. There was a steel girder on the roof and as the driver braked it shot off, hit the ground, flipped over and came straight at

This is Hilda's second Opel Manta; the first being of the original shape which will almost certainly become a classic. They are very simple, well engineered motor cars.

me. I ducked under the scuttle, but the expected crash never came so I surfaced just in time to see it hit the ground level with the windscreen pillar.

I felt there must be something about the Commodore that attracted flying steel missiles and twice was enough for me so I sold it and bought another XJ6. I was not put off Opels and had two secondhand Mantas plus a new automatic Kadett estate car over a period.

When I was able to drive again after breaking my leg I wanted an easy car to drive with automatic, power steering and wide doors to make getting in with my surgical boot easy.

One of my trader friends had just the thing, a Commodore GSE Coupé.

While my left leg was in plaster and a surgical boot I needed an everyday car that was easy to drive; hence this Opel Commodore GSE. The fuel injected engine and impeccable road manners made it a delightful car to drive despite its practicality. I am sure its lovely lines will make it into a "classic" one day and I wish that I had hung on to it.

This was fuel injected and had terrific performance. It was comfortable and easy to drive, just right for the job. I kept it for a while after I was fit again but eventually decided it was surplus to requirements.

Hilda's car had been so satisfactory that her Berlinetta was changed for another one when the time came.

Another deviation from the Jaguar theme was a Rolls Royce MPW Silver Shadow. I had driven a few Shadows, mostly on short journeys, and most confess I didn't like them much apart from the superb engineering, the beautiful interior and the general feeling of quality. There was nothing wrong with the performance either but the handling was dreadful.

Everybody told me that one got used to it, so when this MPW cropped up I decided to give it a try. I did not get used to it. Years of XJ6 motoring had spoiled me for anything floppy and the Rolls started wallowing about if it saw a roundabout in the distance – it didn't wait to get to it! I stuck it for five months and came to the conclusion that, whilst it was a lovely car to own, it was not a nice car to drive. I have since driven several Shadow 2s and Silver Spirits. These have better anti-roll characteristics and rack and pinion steering and the handling, although not up to XJ6 standards, is much better.

Although no longer involved with any form of competitive motoring, both Stephen and I keep up our interest in vintage and historic events, going to Silverstone, Donington and Prescott whenever possible. Having several times spent hours trying to get into and out of Brands Hatch we reckon to leave that one out.

One special occasion for me was when the Goodwood authorities decided to celebrate the 20th anniversary of the track by holding a reunion for everybody who had driven or assisted at the opening meeting in 1948. Hilda came with me and there were lots of people there I hadn't seen for years. A most enjoyable time was had by all.

The highlight of the day was a good blind round the course. It was not supposed to be a blind and to be fair we all started off as if we were out shopping, but inevitably before we got very far it had developed into a jolly good dice. I had a Mk 2 Jaguar in those days which was very suitable for the job, but I don't think Hilda enjoyed it much, her right leg aching through continually pushing an imaginary brake pedal. I hope they hold a 40th reunion in 1988 and hope also I am able to attend.

Classic and vintage car shows such as the Seven Springs Pageant, one-make car club meetings and similar events are one of the bright spots of the present day. Stephen and I attend several during the year but the big indoor shows like Birmingham, Bristol and Brighton do not have the same attraction. There is always a lot of ballyhoo beforehand, but when you get there the most interesting vehicles are the ones in the auction. These are usually superb but only make me wild because I cannot afford them!

Nevertheless they are a good thing for the movement. The organisers must put in an awful lot of work and the success they achieve is well deserved. The FVOC had a stand at Birmingham, in 1984. It took a lot of effort to put it together so I can imagine the amount of hard work and general aggro that the whole thing entailed.

I thoroughly enjoyed the Show itself, but felt it did not reach the standards set by previous Exhibitions. From the pre-Show publicity I expected many more stands. Many of the well-known Clubs were not there, neither were many of the usual specialist car traders whilst the autojumble was a bit of a joke. The cars that were displayed were beautifully turned out and it was nice to be able to walk round without being jostled by crowds. Altogether it was enjoyable, but I did think it would take me longer to cover it all.

This Alvis TD21 was a genuine 46,000 mile car, a little heavy on the steering but otherwise in every respect a lovely car to drive in the vintage tradition. Possibly this was one of the last cars made "like they used to be". As with the Bentley, the Alvis seems to generate a certain respect from other road users whereas with my E-Type I find that I am carved up by every Sierra, Cavalier, BMW and Saab in the South of England.

This is the view given to other road users with the foot down in the Alvis. Both pictures of this car were taken at Claremont Lake, Esher.

As usual there were some mouth-watering cars. Unfortunately my Fairy Godmother had taken two days off, otherwise I'm sure she would have given me the 1750 Alfa-Romeo Zagato two-seater. I kept looking at it, drooling over its beautiful lines and immaculate presentation. My mind went back about 36 years when I used to drive a 2.3-litre eight cylinder version that had been bored out to 2.6. The stupendous performance, precise steering, fantastic brakes coupled with the whine of the supercharger and the general superbly balanced feel of the whole car are memories to treasure.

One very good feature of the Show was the catering. Quite near our Stand was an excellent self-service restaurant where, on the Saturday, I had one of the best curries I've had for some time. On Sunday Stephen and I went to the Griffin, which is just inside the entrance hall. The food was superb, the service friendly and efficient. Thoroughly recommended.

Altogether it was a very friendly Show – well worth seeing and being part of it. We had a drink in the organisers' guest room and the whole atmosphere was one of enthusiasm and goodwill.

We also had a very charming motoring journalist from Sweden who spent a lot of time on our Stand, was most interested in us and was a pleasure to listen to. I'm certain a lot of good came out of it and repeat my previous congratulations and thanks to all concerned.

Another pleasant affair was held at the NAC in Stoneleigh. Apart from the cars there were other attractions and for an outside show there were admirable facilities. The novelty of spending a penny in a galvanised trough behind a screen of sacking wears off after a while! As a result of this meeting we got involved in something else.

The Facel was safely tucked away for the winter in the Isle of Wight, with a short list of jobs to be done by Colin. It had been a much busier summer than I had visualised at the beginning of the year. The Facel had given no trouble and I was well pleased.

Then one evening the telephone rang and a voice said, "This is Bob Cathercole speaking, would you be willing to bring the Facel up to Coventry on the 15th for a big parade?" Such a request could not be ignored so back I went to the IOW. The two preceding days were foggy and I thought about our proposed 5.30 a.m. start. I reckoned Stephen and I would be bleary-eyed enough without fog, but fortunately it turned into a drizzle which, although unpleasant, at least enabled one to see. An effortless purr up the M1 and we arrived in good time for the marshalling of all the cars in the National Agricultural Centre, scene of the recent Town and Country Fair. There were an interesting variety of cars from 1903 onwards, including the odd commercial. In front of us was an immaculate mouth-watering Ferrari Lusso, surely the prettiest Ferrari ever produced.

The usual gathering of vintage machinery was there, some familiar and some we had not previously seen. The morning was cold, damp and miserable. The 8.30 starting time came and went with no sign of any activity ahead. Eventually the Cavalcade began to move and one by one we went out of the gate.

For the first few miles we were able to keep in reasonable order and, in spite of the weather, there were a fair number of people lining the route.

This 1972 MGB roadster is part of my present little "fleet". The photograph is taken in my front garden on the sort of day that is ideal for the car. Although not a "B" fanatic – the car has various well known shortcomings – it is difficult to find for £3500 anything else these days which can give you so much fun while being cheap and easy to maintain. The cheery wave from fellow "B" owners is another desirable feature.

As we came to the outskirts of Coventry the general traffic, crossings, lights, etc., not only stretched the procession out but other cars became interwoven with it. The City was negotiated with no trouble and as we set off for Birmingham the interlopers mostly managed to get away and some sort of order prevailed.

Birmingham was a different kettle of fish. Within a very short time the traffic was snarled up at a rather complicated junction and there we stuck. Sitting in a traffic block is not the Facel's idea of a good time and after a bit I was watching the temperature gauge with some apprehension. The local motorists seemed to be a bit fed up with it and one or two belligerent bus drivers added to the confusion. Eventually we moved off, all was peaceful again and the remainder of the journey was without incident. We were pleased at the interest shown by the locals along the route. Some waved, some cheered and all were obviously enjoying it. We found it interesting and were glad we participated but felt it lasted too long. Not only did it become boring in parts, but not being able to do anything about the effects of several cups of coffee brought anguished expressions to our faces, which no doubt puzzled the spectators who could not see us crossing and uncrossing our legs!

The reception was well-organised with plenty of free beer and plates full of sandwiches. We were directed to park in front of the reception hall with the elite and found ourselves not only with the best cars in the Cavalcade, but in company with three Daimler limousines and a Silver Shadow. These were all resplendent with various coats of arms, fancy registration numbers and chauffeurs, all of which must have set back the local ratepayers a bob or two. Inside, the clinking of mayoral gold chains could be heard above the noise of the peasants drinking their beer. Apart from the weather, it had been an interesting day. The run back in the normal motorway spray was the worst part and, as usual, we got lost trying to find a way of avoiding the North Circular Road.

One of the most unlikely cars to give me a lot of fun was a Vauxhall Viva Estate. I usually ran a small estate car for transporting stuff to or from the Isle of Wight. For some time it was a 13/60 Triumph Herald but one day I saw this Viva for sale. The specification intrigued me so I bought it. It was an HC with a 2,300 cc engine, twin Stromberg carburettors, beefed-up front suspension with wide wheels and tyres. It was a real 'Q' car. The performance was incredible and it handled like a sports car. I could give any MGB a run for its money and enjoyed the look on the faces of other drivers when they couldn't shake off what appeared to be an ordinary Viva.

One day I was coming back from Portsmouth. I expect a lot of you know the stretch of dual carriageway between Hindhead and Milford, a lovely piece of road with several open, sweeping bends. One of them is tighter than it looks and can only be taken fast if there are no other cars about and the correct line is possible.

On this occasion I could see a car in the mirror approaching pretty fast, so I eased up a little and kept to my own side of the road, fully expecting the other car to tuck in behind me. To my horror he did no such thing. The next thing I knew was a Triumph Stag hurtling past me on the outside of the bend and hopelessly placed for getting round it. Somehow he kept it on the road. Either he was an extremely skilled driver, Stag roadholding

This Honda Accord is about the best all round car I have ever owned. It will cruise all day at the legal limit on motorways and is quiet and comfortable under all conditions. With automatic transmission and power steering it is ideal for transport on the congested roads near my home. It also has cruise control but I have never been brave enough to put it to the test.

is better than I thought, or he was just plain lucky. In the back were two little kids who waved at me as he went past.

Another car that belied its looks was an Audi 100 Avant I had for some time. I had driven several Audis, mostly for short distances and thought them alright but not outstanding, but this one was a corker. I sold it to a friend of mine who still has it.

Over the years I have had lots of cars for everyday use and, although it grieves me to say it, many of them have been Japanese. Few people of my generation have any liking for the Japs and we deplore the way they have taken over all our industries, but it is impossible to deny the quality and sound engineering of their products.

This Chevrolet Sportsvan was my transport on a visit to Canada. Its large capacity V8 engine, automatic transmission, power steering and air conditioning made it a natural for their 4 lane freeways. Its manoeuvrability despite large overall size, makes it perfectly practical for use in the Cities too.

For a long time the sort of 'bread and butter' cars we had in for servicing were BMC (later British Leyland), Ford, Triumph, etc., but these gradually were replaced by Datsun, Honda, Colt, Mazda and Toyota. It was quite noticeable how much less attention they required, how clean and free from oil leaks the engines were and they didn't rattle and nothing fell off or broke after a few months.

In the early stages of our Isle of Wight garage I bought three new Viva HC saloons for self-drive hire. They were good little cars. One gave a lot of trouble but they were generally satisfactory. As a result of the troublesome Viva being off the road so much, I bought a second-hand Datsun 1200 as a spare. This car was so popular with the customers that I had to put it in regular use and keep one of the Vivas as a spare. Although it had done a big mileage, nothing ever went wrong with it and when we packed up the hire business it was sold in a flash.

When the new shape Honda Prelude was announced, Hilda's Opel was due for replacement. She liked the look of the Prelude and the local Honda dealer is an old friend of mine so he let me have his first automatic. It will be four years old on April 1st. During this period it has not been touched except for two oil changes. Even the plugs have not been out. At the beginning of winter I fitted a new battery as a precaution but there was still bags of life in the old one. My present runabout is a Toyota Starlet, a delightful little car with a 999cc 12 valve ohc engine, five bearing crankshaft and a five speed gearbox. It is nippy, smooth and quiet and I love it. I would have liked an MG Metro but that engine is basically 35 years old and it is much more expensive.

It took me a long time to persuade Hilda to accept an automatic transmission car but eventually she accepted this Honda Prelude which converted her. Now she will drive nothing else.

Why, oh why, with the complete obliteration of our motor cycle industry as an example did our manufacturers let it happen? Apart from the Opels my 'best' cars have always been British. Never will I change my Jaguar for a Mercedes or BMW and my 'classic' cars are an Alvis and an MG. We can still make the best, so why don't we do it all the time?

One pleasant interlude in the normal routine was a meeting organised by the French Facel Vega Club, the Amicale. It was held at Le Touquet and lasted three days. I no longer had a Facel, so I worked it in with one of my regular trips to Paris, spending a few days there, taking the train to Le Touquet and then hiring a car for the running about. It was a most interesting few days. The Club had organised visits to many places seldom seen by tourists and, needless to say, the meals were fantastic. The Hotel Westminster proved an excellent base and I enjoyed the little Renault hire car. The Amicale has a large membership. I cannot remember ever seeing so many Facels gathered together in one place. Every model was represented by two or three cars, all impeccably presented and a credit to their owners. The airport was still operating a passenger service at the time, so at the end of the festivities I took off in a little turbo prop De Havilland Dove for Gatwick. It was a regular service I had used before. They were cracking little planes and much more to my liking than the big jets.

Meanwhile my friend Dick felt he could once more cope with a manual gearbox, sold his automatic DB6 and asked me to find him another one. By coincidence about the same time a solicitor friend of mine whose Astons I had maintained for many years wanted to sell his DBS6. It was a very nice low mileage car and just the thing for Dick, so I got them together. A big bag of gold changed hands and Dick was in business. It is nice to see these older Astons stay in good hands.

Life at the garage had its interesting moments. I recall an RAF boffin who was quite a nice chap but not backward in airing his technical knowledge. At that time one of the oil additives was the subject of an intense publicity campaign. Full page advertisements in the motoring press proclaimed its virtues in colourful terms. Our boffin friend came in for an oil change and asked for this stuff to be put in. A tin was drawn from the stores, booked out and duly appeared on his invoice, but the mechanic forgot to use it. I left the tin on my desk to remind me to give it to him next time he came in. About a week later he appeared in my office, pointed to the tin before I could say anything and went on about what wonderful stuff it was. His engine was smoother, more lively and was doing an extra 1.2 miles per gallon. I hadn't the heart to tell him. He would have looked such a chump and I felt it was kinder to leave well alone.

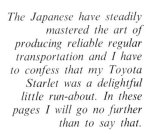

The Japanese have steadily mastered the art of producing reliable regular transportation and I have to confess that my Toyota Starlet was a delightful little run-about. In these pages I will go no further than to say that.

We once towed in a Mini that wouldn't start. Every plug was dripping with oil which seemed odd as the engine was in good shape. We cleaned them, put them back and they promptly oiled up again. Apparently the good lady had decided to check the oil. Never having heard of a dipstick, she removed the filler cap, saw no oil, assumed it was empty and filled it to the top of the valve cover.

MOTs sometimes caused problems. We once failed a Morris 1100 for a split rubber boot on a c/v joint. It came back for re-test, but we found it hadn't been touched. The owner was very indignant because we wouldn't pass it. In high dudgeon he opened the boot and pointed to a nice new rubber surround. After that we always called them gaiters.

At the end of last April my lease ran out. It would have cost a lot of money to renew it and there seemed no point in it. The government was making sure that however hard we worked we didn't make a profit. I was approaching 72 years of age and the oil company intended redeveloping the place anyway. It seemed a good time to turn it in so, reluctantly, I fixed my loyal staff up with other jobs, said goodbye to my customers and shut up shop. I had been there twenty years, and at HWM for the previous twenty. The local paper did a piece entitled: 'Fred's Final Fill-up' recalling an unbroken forty years service to the motoring community. Some of my customers had been with me all that time and as their children grew up I looked after their cars. In three instances the grandchildren became old enough to have cars and so I was looking after three generations of the same families. It was a wrench leaving such a happy environment and I still meet old customers in the street who implore me to go back.

I still enjoy my motoring and now have more time for it. Give me a fine day and my E-Type roadster and I can think of nothing better.

It is nice to look back on the old days. Writing this book has given me a lot of pleasure, but at the same time one must accept changes. There can be no doubt that present day cars have improved beyond recognition since the days of the bull nose Morris. The roads of that period cannot be compared with the network of motorways we now have, the dual carriageways and improved minor roads. It is true the romance has gone out of motoring, but it has also gone out of flying and lots of other pursuits. Whilst people of my age may regret it we must accept it as inevitable.

Although no Y-Type ever visited Brooklands when it was officially in use as a speed circuit, the Y-Type looked perfectly at home parked outside the Club House. Every time I visit Brooklands (this is a gathering of the MGCC) we are blessed with glorious weather so I suppose the old adage about the sun shining on the righteous must have some truth in it after all.

Recently I joined the Brooklands Society. I should have done it years ago but never got around to it although I had attended several of their meetings at the track as a guest. I find these events delightful and full of the right kind of nostalgia, but when I attended the annual dinner I felt only sadness. I seemed to be one of a crowd of old boys desperately trying to revive times that will never return. After all, if we assume a boy would have needed to be at least twelve years old to really appreciate Brooklands and assimilate everything that was going on, there is no-one much under sixty today with

Above: *As I come to the end of my tale I must introduce another shot of my favourite car, the XJ6C. Words cannot do it justice. . .*

As an encore the E-Type appears and takes a final bow.

first hand knowledge of the track. To the others it is just history, something their fathers talked about, something like the war itself which no longer gets the younger generation excited. This doesn't mean we should give it all up. Far from it. We can and should keep the youngsters interested, but mustn't expect them to be as enthusiastic as ourselves.

Looking back on my own motoring career, I can feel nothing but pleasure. There can be little I haven't done and very few cars I haven't driven. I do not take all the credit. I have had the good fortune to often be in the right place at the right time. I have had some wonderful friends, good employers and, above all, good health. I find it incredible that it all started when a rather scruffy little schoolboy went into his local garage and asked for a job.

Motoring is still my main interest in life, both driving and working on my little collection. Unfortunately, it now has to be done at my own expense! My little garage on the Isle of Wight gives me something to worry about and keeps me on my toes.

How lucky can you get?

POSTSCRIPT

T his book was started in 1986 and completed in April 1987. In the two years which have elapsed since completion and publication, several articles and letters have appeared in the specialist magazines that relate to subjects I have written about. Although generally they agree with my own writings, at times they are at variance.

It is difficult for me to comment on this without knowing the background of the writers concerned and the source of their information. I can only say that everything in this book is based on my own experiences and knowledge acquired at first hand. I cannot say fairer than that.

Likewise, over the two year period my own vehicles have changed. The difficulty of carrying out proper maintenance without the garage facilities resulted in the sale of my beloved E-Type and the Series 3 XJ6. The latter always gave me parking problems anyway, owing to its length, so it was exchanged for a Honda Accord Executive. This is a remarkable car. It has everything the Jaguar had, including automatic transmission, power steering, cruise control, air conditioning, electric windows, etc. It is as much at home cruising on the motorways as it is doing the shopping and it never goes wrong.

An MGB roadster (chrome bumpers) has now joined the stable to replace the E Type. Not in the same class, of course, but lots of fun and far more practical for everyday use. My faithful XJ6 Coupé is still my favourite motor car.

The Toyota Starlet was sold in April 1988. It was a company car and when the Chancellor raised the company car tax yet again it no longer made economic sense to pay extra income tax on it when I had four cars of my own. I consider this tax grossly unfair anyway. Living near Heathrow, I have lots of friends who work there. They all get free or very cheap flights all over the world. The miners get free coal, the railway workers free travel. These are more of a 'perk' than a company car, which at least is used partly for business, but if told to pay extra tax they would all go on strike.

Other things have cropped up too. I mentioned the HWM Coupé we built from parts and wondered if it still existed. In the September issue of *Classic and Sportscar* there is an item concerning it and a picture of it lapping Montlhéry at the June Age d'Or meeting. It would appear it is now owned by Pierre Lagarde, but there is no clue as to where it is based.

A request in the *MG Enthusiast* magazine for information regarding the two K3s I raced brought forth a very detailed reply from Mike Hawke of the MG Car Club Triple M Register. It appears both cars survive, both in the U.S.A. Apparently BLT 703 came 4th at Le Mans in 1934, driven by Roy Eccles and Charlie Martin. AGW 37 was driven by Miss Enid Riddel to a class win in the 1934, 1935 and 1938 Paris-St Raphael Rally and she also made ftd in several hill climbs.

I am greatly indebted to Mike Hawkes for this information, which is typical of the splendid enthusiasm to be found in the MG Car Club. I always enjoy their meetings more than those of any other club I belong to. They are always lucky with the weather too!

I have also had interesting correspondence with Winston Goodfellow, President of the Iso and Bizzarini Owners Club in the U.S.A. He is obviously a keen and knowledgeable man when it comes to Isos and his enthusiasm for these cars comes through in his letters.

In Chapter 10 I mention the twenty year anniversary meeting at Goodwood and express the hope there will be another one in 1988, but 1988 is now past us and they didn't hold one.

Perhaps we will have one in 1998 to celebrate the fiftieth anniversary. I wonder what sort of lap times I will record in an electric wheel chair! I am sure I will think of some other things before this book reaches the bookshops but I must stop somewhere or this addendum will become another chapter.

APPENDIX 1: CARS I HAVE OWNED

Jaguar/Daimler

Mark 1	1
Mark 2	2
S Type	2
420	2
XJ6 Series 1	4
XJ6 Series 2	4
XJ6 Series 3	1
V12 E Type	2
XJS	1
V8 250	1
Total Jaguar	20

Austin

7	3
8	2
10	1
12/6	1
14/6	1
Total Austin	8

Bentley

3½ Ltr.	1
Mk 6	1
R Type	1
S Type	2
T Type	1
Total Bentley	6

Opel

Kadett	1
Manta	3
Commodore	2

Vauxhall

Viva	2
Victor	1
Total Vauxhall	3

Rover

Ten	1
Twelve	1
Total Rover	2

Alvis

Speed 25	1
TD 21	1
Total Alvis	2

MG

YB Saloon	1
B GT & Roadster	2
Total MG	3

One each of:

Triumph Herald
BSA 10
Wolseley Hornet 6
Singer 1½ Ltr. Le Mans
Rolls Royce MPW
Humber Snipe
Mazda 328
Honda Civic
Facel Vega HK500
Oldsmobile 6
Datsun Cherry

Total Opel	6	Hillman Minx	
		Audi 100 5S	
Morris		Toyota Starlet	
Eight	2		
Minor	1		
Oxford	1		
Mini	2		
Total Morris	6		
Ford			
Eight	2		
Prefect	1		
Escort	1		
Fiesta	1		
Total Ford	5	Total to date	75

APPENDIX 2: CARS I CAN REMEMBER HAVING DRIVEN

Austin
Alta
Austro-Daimler
Alfa Romeo
Alvis
Ascot
Aston Martin
Adler
AJS
Audi
AC
Allard
Auburn
Bentley
Borgward
Buick
Belsize Bradshaw
BSA
Ballot
Bugatti
Bristol
Brocklebank
BMW
Bianchi
Bond
Chrysler
Cadillac
Calcott
Citroen
Clyno
Calthorpe
Colt
Cord
Chevrolet
Crossley
Daimler
Dodge
Delage
DAF

Fiat
Ford
Graham
Gilbern
Gwynne
Graham Paige
Humber
Hillman
HE
Honda
HRG
Hyundai
Hotchkiss
HWM
Hudson
Healey
Iso Rivolta
Imperia
Isotta Fraschini
Isetta
Invicta
Jaguar
Jensen
Jowett
Lagonda
Lotus
Lamborghini
Lincoln
Lancia
La Salle
Lanchester
Lea Francis
Marmon
MG
Morris
Mazda
Marauder
Maserati
Morgan

Rolls Royce
Renault
Rover
Railton
Riley
Reliant
Raleigh 3 wheeler
Standard
Simca
SS
Sunbeam
Studebaker
Singer
Swift
Saab
Salmson
Skoda
Suzuki
Talbot
Triumph
Toyota
Vauxhall
Voisin
Vale
Volkswagen
Volvo
Wolseley
Willys Knight

Commercial Vehicles*

Bedford
Dodge
Morris Commercial
Leyland
AEC

Delahaye	Mercedes	Thornycroft
DKW	Moscovitch	Albion
Datsun	Nash	Dennis
De Soto	Oldsmobile	Star
Darracq	Opel	Austin
Erskine	Panhard	Chevrolet
ERA	Plymouth	
Essex	Peerless	* Heavy stuff, not
Facel Vega	Pontiac	including commercial
Falcon Knight	Packard	derivatives of cars
Ferrari	Porsche	
Frazer Nash	Peugeot	

Total: 130

Appreciation

Photographs frequently come down over the years in a form which makes it difficult or impossible to accurately trace their origin. If there are within these pages any such unacknowledged illustrations, I extend my apologies and thanks to the photographer or artist concerned.

INDEX